THE DELUSION OF SOVEREIGNTY

Would independence weaken Québec?

Kimon Valaskakis Ph D is full professor of economics at Université de Montréal, founding-president of the GAMMA Institute and founding-partner of the international strategic management firm ISOGROUP CONSULTANTS. The British newsweekly *The Economist* described him as "one of Canada's most perceptive thinkers." He appears frequently in the media and through his writings in the disciplines of forecasting and strategic planning. He is the author of eight books and sixty scientific articles.

Angéline Fournier LL M is vice-president of the GAMMA Institute and a consultant with ISOGROUP CONSULTANTS. Trained as a jurist, she holds a Master of Business Law from Université de Paris V and a Master of Law from McGill University, and has been admitted to the Bar of Paris. She has studied moreover at the Centre des Communautés Européennes in Paris. As a consultant and researcher, she has worked actively for several years in the area of social, economic and political forecasting, publishing in Canada, the United States and France. She frequently writes about her field of specialization and is co-author of a book about Quebec.

The GAMMA Institute is a non-partisan forecasting think-tank described by the Paris daily newspaper *Le Monde* as "a centre of international renown." Based in Montreal and supported by an international network of researchers, the Institute analyzes broad social trends, builds alternative scenarios and works closely with ISOGROUP CONSULTANTS, providing a bridge between forecasting and strategic planning.

KIMON VALASKAKIS / ANGÉLINE FOURNIER

THE DELUSION OF SOVEREIGNTY

Would independence weaken Québec?

translated from French by George Tombs

Robert Davies Publishing
MONTREAL—TORONTO

This book may be ordered in Canada from

General Distribution Services,
☎1-800-387-0141 / 1-800-387-0172 FAX 1-416-445-5967;
in the U.S.A., dial toll-free 1-800-805-1083;

or call the publisher, toll-free throughout North America:
1-800-481-2440, FAX (514)481-9973.

The publisher takes this opportunity to thank the
Canada Council and the *Ministère de la Culture du Québec*
for their continuing support.

Table of Contents

PREFACE

At a time when our society is facing tough questions and challenges, the GAMMA Institute, a non-partisan forecasting think-tank, wanted to make a contribution to the debate. We have undertaken to study whether independence would be suitable for the future of Quebec, as it approaches the threshold of the third millenium. The GAMMA Institute could not remain outside of the debate, since its mission is the critical analysis of trends, the explanation of possible and/or desirable futures, and the alternative paths by which to arrive at them. The GAMMA Institute has never expressed political opinions and does not plan to do so in the future. Indeed, it has always encouraged its researchers to develop very divergent and sometimes even contradictory points of view. Its special strength is in encouraging thinkers and men and women of action to "see the big picture" and "see far ahead" by using an interdisciplinary approach and long-term analysis. Consequently, the views expressed in this book are not those of the Institute but rather those of the authors, who speak in their capacity as concerned citizens, proud to take part in the debate that concerns all of us. As Seneca said: "There is no such thing as a favorable wind for the man who doesn't know where he is going." All Quebeckers should take part in the debate; they should critically examine all aspects of the problem, and decide once and for all what their future position will be.

This book does not hide its colors. It is a plea against Quebec independence, based on an analysis of the indépendantistes' ten most widespread and most frequently-quoted myths. We highlight the weaknesses and indeed the analytical errors we detect in the thinking of those who advocate the independence of Quebec. These errors can be divided into three groups. In a first category of "diagnostic" errors, certain erroneous beliefs lead to an analysis of the past and the future that is simply out of touch with reality. An example is the belief that Quebec does not benefit and has never benefitted from being a part of

Canada. In a second category of "predictive" errors, superficial diagnostics lead to frivolous conclusions, such as the belief held by indépendantistes that English Canada will have no choice but to make important concessions in the hopes of maintaining an economic union with an independent Quebec. Lastly, in a third category of "strategic" errors, the problem may have been adequately defined, but the solutions chosen are completely inappropriate. This is particularly striking in the analysis made of the French fact in North America and of strategies required to promote the French language. In a study commissioned by the Conseil de la langue française in the 1980s, GAMMA Institute researchers concluded that the French language did indeed face a significant threat in North America. But they concluded at the time, as we still conclude today, that independence would be the worst strategy, if the goal is protecting the French language and culture of Quebec. Even though indépendantistes have succeeded in identfying the problem, they are committing a grave error in advocating the "French here, English everywhere else" approach. These three categories of errors are to be found in the most common arguments in favor of indepence.

We would like to thank our researchers and particularly Yannis Philopoulos and Steve Wishart. We would like to thank all those who helped bring this ambitious project to fruition, particularly Aurèle Beaulnes, Dr. Yves Rabeau and Dr. Daniel Seni.

We present the positions in this book in a spirit of openness to all readers, whether federalist, autonomist, associationist, separatist, indépendantiste or undecided. Our critique is hard-hitting. Even so, we welcome serious responses from those who might wish to make them, as part of the debate which the citizens will need in order to make their choice with full knowledge of the facts.

Kimon Valaskakis and Angéline Fournier
Montreal, December 1994

INTRODUCTION
National "sovereignty" on the threshold of the third millenium

WHAT IS "SOVEREIGNTY?"

Masters of our own destiny
Symbolic sovereignty
Legal sovereignty
Real sovereignty

THE BACKGROUND: AN EVER-CHANGING WORLD

Understanding globalization
Understanding the counter-trends
Conclusion

WHAT IS SOVEREIGNTY?

Masters of our own destiny?

In the mid-1970s, the American musical comedy "Stop the world, I want to get off!" was a big hit on Broadway. It responded to a deep-seated feeling among many people that the world was getting far too complicated. The mid-1970s were rocked by the energy crisis, stagflation, fears about growing pollution, the dangers of the Cold War, terrorism, etc. All the bad news was taking a heavy toll on people. It was a time of "dropouts," protest movements and challenges to the consumer society.

Each period of history has its own protest movements. Nowadays, in the 1990s, the complexity of our way of life leaves us with much the same feeling as people had twenty years ago. Individuals today are grappling with forces beyond their control, and they are losing their autonomy. We are fed up with the crisis of unemployment; with a recession we are only beginning to come out of; with the indebtedness of the State - something that is difficult to get under control; with widespread budget cuts that offer no apparent benefits; with the shrinking social-security net and growing poverty. We want to break away, be "masters of our own destiny." It's our modern way of reliving the "dropout" movement of the 1970s.

What form should be given to this contemporary desire to escape - as well as to control our destiny in a world cast adrift? The answer to the question varies from place to place. Contemporary history abounds in examples ranging from the peaceful to the destructive. "Peaceful" illustrations of the need to control one's destiny include the "friendly divorce" of the Czechs and Slovaks, which, as we will see later on, was not quite painless, and the democratic drive for independence. The Quebec independence movement is particularly interesting in this respect, since it took on new vigor at the beginning of the 1990s, when it was becoming clear that states no longer had as much room for manoeuvre as in years past. Of course, some people claim that Canada's constitutional debate was the final

11

blow. It is conceivable, however, that a completely different kind of malaise set in during the constitutional debate, leading to the resurgence of the independence movement in Quebec: the fact that states were losing control over the solutions they could find for the increasingly complex problems experienced by our modern societies.

In other countries, the need for autonomy as well as the desire to chart a new course and to protect society from "bad influences" are unfortunately expressed in violent ways. Religious fundamentalism and ethnic fanaticism are illustrated by the struggle of Muslim fundamentalists against the "Great Satan," whether that Satan be American (in the case of Iranian fundamentalists) or foreign (in the case of fundamentalists in Egypt and Algeria, where a fundamentalist minority ordered a series of assassinations of foreigners.) In Rwanda in 1994, being a Tutsi in Hutu territory or a Hutu in Tutsi territory amounted to a death sentence. The former Yugoslavia has been devastated by ethnic struggles and generalized violence.

In each of these cases, one can find a growing desire for autonomy, a desire to control one's destiny and to chart a course in a world cast adrift.

In Quebec, this desire has led to a resurgence of the "independence" movement, which promotes the "sovereignty" of Quebec. "Sovereignty" is a vague word, creating difficulties even for experts. To get a full grasp of the concept would take university degrees in at least four disciplines: political science, international law, international economy and social psychology. Indeed, in some cases, sovereignty refers to the exercise of power, or the sharing of power and responsibilities within the structure of the State, whereas in other cases it is the world environment that determines the areas where sovereignty can be exercised. Some aspects of the Quebec sovereignty project have to do with symbols, culture and social history. The exact meaning of the word "sovereignty" is hard to nail down. That is why it has been used in so many different ways over the last twenty years. Some people see it as a remedy - even the ultimate remedy - for all ills, as a *deus ex machina* ready to jolt society out of its current slump. We propose to start off by demystifying the concept, by interpreting it in three distinct ways: "symbolic" sovereignty, "legal" sovereignty and "real" sovereignty.

Symbolic sovereignty

Authority is at the very heart of the idea of sovereignty. According to the *Dictionnaire canadien de la langue française,* sovereignty is defined as "absolute authority, a final decision, total power." To be sovereign means to be "supreme, perfect, excellent." The idea has roots in the historical doctrine of the divine right of kings, according to which the right to rule derives from God and kings are answerable for their actions to God alone. Louis XIV, for example, used this concept to justify his famous declaration: "L'Etat c'est moi" - "I am the State." It is therefore not surprising that kings should call themselves "sovereigns," although in our day they exercise mostly symbolic sovereignty and have very little real authority.

In the world today, there are just over two hundred states claiming to be "sovereign." Less than fifty of them have real authority over the principal problems facing them. The vast majority of states are dependent on external events, without having any control over those events. Nevertheless, these states have all the trappings of sovereignty: presidential palaces, flags, national anthems, embassies, border posts with uniformed guards, etc. Prince Rainier is the undisputed sovereign of Monaco, which is not part of France and has a distinct tax system reduced to a strict minimum (the principality lives mainly off the economic benefits generated by the famous Casino of Monte Carlo). The subjects of the Prince are citizens of Monaco. The Principality has no army and is totally dependent on the infrastructure of France. Indeed, there are no real borders between the two countries. France could cut off the water and electricity supply of Monaco tomorrow if it wanted to, and send a small detachment of policemen to take over the principality without further ado. Yet the extremely picturesque pomp, circumstance and symbolism associated with the sovereign remain intact, like something out of a Gilbert and Sullivan musical comedy.

Some analysts suggest that the sovereignty ultimately being sought by Quebeckers would above all be symbolic and would change nothing apart from government protocol. On this assumption, the Quebec people would be no more sovereign than the current Queen of England, undisputed "sovereign" of Canada, or than the "Sovereign State of Georgia" or the "Sovereign Commonwealth of Massachusetts" in the United States. Some American states even have a secessionist clause in their constitutions, confirming that they are "sovereign" states within the United States and have the right to leave the union on request. Vermont has a charming tradition calling for an occasional plebiscite allowing the citizens to reassess their place in the United States. But every student of history knows what happened when some American states actually tried to separate from the American federation. The Civil War took care of the problem once and for all, by establishing that the American federation is indivisible and secessionists are considered traitors. Countries can indulge in the luxury of flags, national anthems and the ornaments of state. But it is possible to be "sovereign" without having a hope of influencing the course of events in the world or changing anything in the practical life of society.

Legal sovereignty

Legal sovereignty brings us into the field of the precedence of institutions, laws and rules. When two or more legislative bodies take a position on a given subject, which one has the last word? The "sovereign" body is that which takes the final decision. In 1990, the debate over the Meech Lake Accord touched on this question. If the "distinct society clause" of Quebec had taken precedence over the "Canadian Charter of Rights and Freedoms," the National Assembly of Quebec could have invoked this precedence in order to legislate in a sovereign fashion. If the

Charterhas taken precedence, however, things would have ended up the other way round. The question never got an answer, and was one of the main reasons the Meech Lake Accord failed.

It should be noted that claims to legal precedence can be "contagious." The last months of the Soviet Union were marked by ever-increasing claims that particular legal authorities should take precedence over others. The Parliament of the Russian Republic wanted precedence over the Soviet Parliament, while the regional Parliaments of the Russian Republic wanted precedence over the decisions of the Parliament in Moscow. This infernal centrifual movement led to the splintering of the Soviet Union. In Canada, the Mohawk crisis of 1990 and the failed Charlottetown Accord of 1992 gave an idea what the spiral of ever-increasing claims can be like. A key question remains unanswered to this day: if Quebec becomes sovereign, how can the Mohawks, Cree and Innu be prevented from wanting their own sovereignty? And how can other "separations within separation" be prevented?

It is worth pointing out that the concept of federalism itself recognizes the notion of shared sovereignty, as we will see later on. The federal government has the last word in some areas, the provincial governments in others, and both levels of government share some areas of sovereignty. As a result, provincial governments are "sovereign" when their decisions are final, and in other cases the central government has the last word.

Real sovereignty

Just how far can "legal sovereignty" go? Rather than answer that question, indépendantistes get carried away in a flood of passion that is out of touch with reality. The way some politicians talk, it seems as if the fate of the world were determined in one of two places: Ottawa or Quebec. Quebeckers are being called upon to create a new country, as if we were lucky winners in a lottery, as if we could use unlimited funds to choose and decorate a new house. Should we choose paint or wall-paper, modern or antique furnishings, a carpet or oak flooring? It is simply an illusion to suppose that Quebec has multiple choices - an illusion both charming and unrealistic. In actual fact, most things in this world are determined neither in Ottawa nor in Quebec. Sure, King Canute was sovereign, but he could not turn back the sea. Some waves of change are well beyond the jurisdiction of the Canadian Parliament or the National Assembly of Quebec, whether those legislative bodies are considered sovereign or not.

Implicit in the idea of "real" sovereignty is the actual exercise of power in a number of areas. Unless the state that claims to be sovereign can bring influence to bear on the debates affecting it, its sovereignty is a merely symbolic one, nourished by psycho-social illusions. That is why the underlying question of this book is as follows: Given the context of globalization, the rise of global interdependence and the weakening of small nation-states, is Quebec independence the best way to fulfil the legitimate aspirations of Quebeckers and to improve their well-being? Will independence increase Quebec's room for manoeuvre and its real ability to direct its own future?

In 1980, the collective answer given by Quebeckers to this question was No. In 1995, after making a detailed study of the question, we are convinced that the interests of Quebec will best be served by saying No once again. Our conclusion is reinforced by an objective analysis of the world environment, which has created both constraints and opportunities for Quebec. We hold that the aspirations of Quebeckers are perfectly legitimate, but that it is completely unrealistic to choose independence in order to fulfil these aspirations. Within Canada, there are many other more effective and direct ways of bringing about the best aspects of Quebec's vision for society. Resorting to independence strikes us as useless, outmoded, and even hazardous for the development of Quebec society, which will have fewer real choices, less real power and a truncated sovereignty.

We will start by sketching the background of the new world order in 1995, in order to analyze the opportunities and constraints created by that order. After that, we will take a careful and critical look at the ten myths most frequently used to promote Quebec independence. In most cases, these myths are the result of diagnostic errors, sophistic arguments and die-hard myths. We invite the reader to read our analysis with an open mind.

THE BACKGROUND:
AN EVER-CHANGING WORLD

UNDERSTANDING GLOBALIZATION

The rise of global interdependence

A cursory glance at the state of the planet in 1995 leads us to an inescapable conclusion: namely, that to believe an independent Quebec would be "sovereign" is simply to fly in the face of the growing interdependence of states brought about by globalization. Some people consider "globalization" to be a cliché. It refers nevertheless to a reality, characterized by the rise of global interdependence and the transformation of the planet Earth into a "global village," as Marshall McLuhan put it. What are the key elements of this "global village?"

First of all, there has been a revolution in the field of telecommunications, creating a worldwide electronic network, commonly called the Information Superhighway. This superhighway has two "lanes." The first consists of a coaxial-cable and fibre-optic network, while the second consists of a digital telephone network. Together, they make it possible to transmit voice, data and images over long distances, whether by cable or hertzian waves. Everyone can plug into the Information Superhighway round-the-clock, anywhere in the world, by using a miniature, personalized cellular telephone.

The telecommunications revolution has been accompanied by the less spectacular but nonetheless real evolution of transportation, particularly air transportion, which has shortened distances around the globe. According to the OECD, 50 % of world trade is carried on by air. Products from far afield are now transported to local markets by cargo aircraft. Individuals can travel by air from one end of the planet to the other. The concept of closed markets no longer exists. Everyone can compete with everyone.

Moreover, in the "global village" of telecommunications and transportion, pollution makes a mockery of national boundaries, which it crosses without either a visa or a passport. The thinning of the ozone layer is a planetary phenomenon. The reheating of the world's atmosphere cannot be stopped by a unilateral declaration of sovereignty. Climatologists even claim that the fluttering of butterfly wings in the tropical forests of Africa can affect rainfall in North America. Whether one likes it or not, the "ecological" planet is practically indivisible and we have to come to terms with planetary environmental interdependence, even if the Constitution of a given country assigns that jurisdiction to a provincial government.

The men and women of all countries in the world now have a common destiny, thanks to the increase of global interdependence in the areas of geopolitical security (the Gulf Crisis in 1990-91), of radioactive fallout (Three Mile Island and Chernobyl), of the transmission of disease (AIDS, cholera, colds etc.) or even of culture (television viewers the world over watch the same programs, such as the World Cup, the Olympics, American TV series).

The globalization of production and the rise of the Stateless Corporation

The economic nature of the phenomenon of interdependence has more to do with the globalization of "production" than with that of "markets." The rise of international trade on a planetary scale is not new. Already, at the close of the nineteenth century, the North Atlantic, with its European and North American shores, constituted the centre of the world. Gravitating around this axis, the colonial territories of Africa and Asia boosted the industrialization of the metropolis by providing it with raw materials.

But nowadays, the globalization of production is bringing about a new division of labor, which profoundly alters production relationships. From 1850 to 1970, world specialization was situated at the level of products. Each country specialized in the production of particular goods, and sought its compara-

19

tive advantage at the level of relative costs. But over the last twenty years, product specialization has been gradually replaced by product-component specialization. Automobiles, for example, are increasingly becoming a form of "stateless" merchandise. The components can come from several places around the world. Some Hondas manufactured in Ohio have more American components than some Chryslers, whose components come from Japan. As a result, the expressions "made in Canada, the United States, France, etc." are losing their meaning because of the globalization of production processes.

Meanwhile, the transportation and communications revolutions are transforming the multinational corporation - the causal agent of the globalization of production - into a virtually stateless entity. It is now possible to have a delocalization of production on a planetary scale. The subsidiaries of multinationals specialize in the components of products that come from every corner of the world, and can then be assembled at a centrepoint. Some fifty per cent of "international" trade within the "Triad" comprising Europe, North America and Southeast Asia is actually trade between the subsidiaries of multinational corporations. Production factors (labor, capital, resources and technology) are becoming ever more mobile and leap over national boundaries.

The more technical the principal factors of an industry are, the more the industry is mobile, since computer hardware and software and above all grey matter have the least trouble leaping over national boundaries. World corporations take their industrial-location decisions on the basis of profitability and much less so on the basis of economic nationalism. Since financial decisions are objective and not sentimental, a Quebec company might decide, without the slightest difficulty, to move its factories to Mexico in order to lower production costs, even if its president favored Quebec independence. The larger a corporation gets, the more stateless it becomes: its products are stateless, its senior executives are international, its shareholders are international holding companies and the site of its head office is selected for fiscal reasons, rather than cultural or nationalist ones.

The weakening of small nation-states

The rise of stateless corporations is both the cause and the result of the globalization of production. This also has a devastating effect on the room for manoeuvre and the effective power of small nation-states. In an open system, where production factors move about at will, the corporation and "globalized" entrepreneurs can brandish the threat of imminent departure, if they are dissatisfied with the policies of a government, even if that government is their own. This permanent threat hangs like the Sword of Damocles over the head of all governments, especially those in small states, that are therefore required to double their efforts to attract and retain mobile corporations, sometimes at the cost of significant fiscal concessions. The globalization of production means that governments are losing power, because of the growing gap that seems to be opening up: the gap between the economic space in which increasingly planetary corporations operate and the space of political jurisdiction of governments, hemmed in by national or provincial boundaries.

This loss of governmental power shows up moreover in the evaluation of annual budgets. Once the Minister of Finance has tabled the budget, the question is less how voters react than how "financial markets" react, since they are in a position to punish delinquent governments with massive capital flight. Every day, a trillion dollars travel around the planet, in search of maximum profits, via the Information Superhighway. Governments can do little more than go with the flow and try to profit from the waves. As for "big" governments, even they can find themselves stripped of the power to intervene. A cut-throat attack on the U.S. dollar by one trillion dollars of mobile capital could not possibly be thrown back by the Federal Reserve Bank. The concerted efforts of the central banks of the G7 countries could not hold back a wage of speculative attacks. The threat of corporate departures and the nightmarish vision of capital flight end up significantly reducing the effective power of all governments and make the concept of sovereignty seem all the more symbolic.

UNDERSTANDING THE COUNTER-TRENDS

Because of the explosive upheaval of globalization, many societies are concerned and are rightly asking themselves fundamental questions. The response of "Stop the world, I want to get off," mentioned above, is hardly irrational. The threat of being carried off by winds one cannot control does indeed contribute to insecurity. The desire to chart a distinctive course and use one's compass is commendable. But which course and which compass? Around the world today, five counter-trends are developing in response to the all-pervasive effects of globalization:

(1) the resurgence of the nation-state, a model much in fashion in Eastern Europe;

(2) the rise of religious fundamentalism in Muslim countries;

(3) decentralizing pressures within nation-states;

(4) the move toward European-style and American-style "continentalization;"

(5) political and social globalization, which is pushing for a some future planetary government.

The nationalist response: from dreams to reality

East of the Oder-Neisse line, the border between Germany and Poland, people have rediscovered the joys and vicissitudes of extreme nationalism. The former members of the COMECON long stumbled under the Soviet yoke. They have celebrated their liberation by embracing both the capitalist market and an advanced form of tribalism.

The Soviet Union splintered into republics each of which planned to have its own currency, institutions, immigration policies, etc. Some of these republics even inherited a nuclear arsenal. And since none of them has an ethnically homogeneous population, tribal conflicts are turning into conflicts within and outside of the republics. At any moment war can break out between Armenia and Azerbaijan, or between Muslims and Christians of other republics. The Chechens want to separate without the consent of Russia and the havoc created by the disintegration of the USSR is so traumatic that some people predict a return to a totalitarian regime, whether of the right or the left, and the eventual reconstitution of the Russian empire.

The "Yugoslav model" was once upheld as an extremely interesting system of comanagement. But the former Yugoslavia has since thrown itself into a frenzy of ethnic and religious massacres. The people of Serbia, Croatia, Bosnia, Skopje, etc. have been in conflict for three years now, despite the presence of United Nations peacekeepers. The situation for men, women and children is catastrophic. The outburst of nationalism seems uncontrollable.

The friendly divorce experienced by the former Czechoslovakia is more interesting. People have referred to it as the "quiet separation" and the "velvet divorce" - some even going so far as to say it constitutes a promising example for Canada. Actually, this separation has created many problems; in practice it has not turned out at all the way it was supposed to be in theory. What does this breakup teach us? We can identify six lessons to be drawn from this experience:

1. The threat of separation, even if used as a negotiation strategy, can "accidentally" lead to divorce

In Slovakia, independence came about without the support of the majority of the population. In July 1992, 49 % of Slovaks favored maintaining either federal links or a unitary Czechoslovak state, while 46 % wanted either a confederation (30 % wanted a sort of sovereignty-association) or straight independence (16 % wanted a republic). But the Slovaks hoped to wrench constitutional concessions away from the Czechs. That is how a majority of Slovaks ended up voting for federal and provincial parties that advocated a breakup of the federation.

The separation of the country in two became inevitable when the Czech federal government let the Slovaks separate.

2. Even after a "quiet" separation, sovereignty-association is hard to bring about

Many Slovaks favored a sort of confederal arrangement with the Czech Republic. But judging from the Czechoslovak experience, that seems hard to bring about. The Slovaks wanted a sort of sovereignty-assocation (with shared currency, defence and foreign policy, as well as coordinating political institutions). But the Czech government offered the Slovaks two choices: either help build a federation that works or formally leave the federation by separating. The Czechs preferred a complete breakup of the country, in order to finish once and for all with endless constitutional quarrels that had rocked the federation since the downfall of the communist regime. (*Economist Intelligence Unit,* 1992:10).

The Slovaks never thought the Czechs would let them leave; after underestimating their partners, the Slovaks are now prisoners of their own strategy, for better or worse. Ten months after the breakup, an opinion poll revealed that, had there been a referendum, 60 % of Slovaks would have voted against independence and 23 % for the breakup. (*Economist Intelligence Unit,* 1994a:28).

3. After separation, it is much more difficult than believed to maintain an integrated economic space with a joint currency and customs union

Is it possible to keep a joint currency, a customs union and bilateral trade intact after separation? Some people in Quebec say it is possible. The Czechoslovak experience suggests that is little more than wishful thinking.

The Czechoslovak economic space disintegrated very rapidly after independence. The two countries quickly came to the conclusion that it was impossible to maintain a monetary union with a joint currency. In fact, without the coordinating mechanism of an economic union resulting from a political union, the two states were going to have to adopt vastly different economic policies, making a single coherent monetary policy impossible. As a result, the Slovaks and Czechs agreed to keep the Czechoslovak currency for six months, before issuing their own separate currencies.

But the monetary union only lasted six weeks. The prospect of a breakup of the monetary union and the likely devaluation of the new Slovak currency created a national and international crisis of confidence in the value of the Czechoslovak crown. Czech commercial banks converted their crowns for more stable foreign currency. Consequently, the reserves of the Czech National Bank shrank by $270 million (37 %) in the two weeks following the breakup. Foreign banks with large quantities of Czechoslovak crowns sold them all and refused to buy any more. The Czech government quickly came to the conclusion that it was time to bring an end to the monetary union and to issue a new, more dependable currency. That is how the two countries dropped their joint currency on Feb. 8, five months before they planned to.

The customs union collapsed soon after separation, even though the two republics had wanted to create a customs union with joint tariff policies and a free-trade zone. Currently, many customs posts along the Czech-Slovak border control the flow of goods, services and people. The two countries accuse one another of having thrown up many non-tariff barriers.

Both republics experienced a major drop in trade and slowing economic growth, once the federation broke up and the customs union fell apart. In January 1993, one month after the breakup, trade was down by 60 % (compared to the monthly average of the previous year). That had a disastrous effect on the economies of the two countries.

It has been estimated that the Gross Domestic Product of Slovakia dropped by 7 % immediately after separation. In economic terms, that amounts to a major depression. By comparison, during two deep recessions in Quebec, the GDP declined by 1.5 % in 1981-82 and by 2 % in 1990-91.

In the Czech Republic, in the three months following separation, industrial production declined by 4.9 %, construction activity took an 11.0 % dive and railway movements were down 31.4 % (*Economist Intelligence Unit,* 1993 b:7). In 1993, Czech exports to Slovakia plunged 30 %. The Czech government calculated that every 10 % drop in exports to Slovakia translated into a 1.0 % decline in the GDP and a 0.5 % drop in tax revenues. According to estimates by the Economist Intelligence Unit, separation brought on a decline in the Czech GDP in 1993 of between 2.0 % and 2.5 %. (*Economist Intelligence Unit,* 1994 c:7).

Little hard information is available about the economic situation in Slovakia. Even so, it is clear there was a significant decline in industrial production during the first four months after separation and a huge drop in Slovak exports headed for the Czech Republic. This decline in trade had a devastating effect on the Slovak economy. In 1992, the year before the breakup, exports amounted to 68 % of Slovakia's GDP. Half of those exports were headed for the Czech Republic. In spite of a 10.4 % devaluation of Slovak currency in July 1993, Slovak exports did not rise. The combined effect of a drop in trade and depressed domestic demand sent Slovakia's GDP into a 7 % nosedive in 1993. (*Economist Intelligence Unit,* 1994 c:7).

4. Dividing up federal assets and debts after separation was a bitter experience

Slovakia's separatist leaders tried to reassure the Slovak people prior to independence that separation would be friendly, polite and rational. They claimed that the Czechs were rational people and that dividing up the federation's debt would not present any problems. However, these assurances turned out to be hollow.

Once the two republics split up, the division of federal assets and debts was hotly debated and many disagreements arose over:

— federal buildings and gold reserves located in Prague;

— federal government-controlled companies, such as the Czechoslovak national airline;

— the accumulation of debts that Slovak banks contracted with the Czech Republic in 1992. (*Economist Intelligence Unit,* 1993 c:19).

This last point became a bone of contention for the two partners for the following reason: as soon as it became clear the Slovaks were becoming indebted to the Czech Republic, the latter decided to freeze 22 million shares acquired by Slovak citizens during the first wave of privatizations in 1992, until such time as the Slovaks paid off their debts. This conflict became highly political, since neither party wanted to make any compromises and the deadline set for dividing up federal property, April 15, had to be extended. (*Economist Intelligence Unit,* 1993 b:33).

5. Independence brings about the deterioration of public finances and a rise in the cost of public services

Slovak leaders claimed, much like some Quebec leaders, that the independence of Slovakia would result in significant savings. Once again, this assurance proved hollow.

Slovakia's public finances quickly deteriorated after separation. The budget deficit shot up from Sk 1.2 billion at the end of February 1993 to Sk 12 billion three months later: a rise of 1000 % in just three months!!! According to the Slovak Minister of Finance, the spectacular rise in the deficit is due to the cost of creating new ministries, such as the Ministries of Defence and Foreign Affairs and the Ministry of the Interior. Moreover, the cost of setting up new embassies and creating a new currency cost the Slovak treasury dearly in the first three months of independence. The cost of some public services also rose substantially during the four months after the Czechoslovak federation splintered: the price of bus tickets rose 29 %, while train tickets and telephone calls went up 50 % (*Economist Intelligence Unit,* 1993 b:36-37).

6. Ethnic nationalism leads to problems with minorities inhabiting the territory of the new state

The anti-Czech and anti-Hungarian character of Slovak nationalism, embraced by various Slovak political parties, forced the Czechs to abandon any hope of reaching an agreement with the Slovaks in a renewed federation. At the same time, the Hungarian minority in Slovakia felt more comfortable in a multiethnic federation than in a state based on Slovak nationalism; for this reason, the Hungarian minority bitterly opposed separation.

Language policies in Slovakia and the treatment of the Hungarian minority there led to major tension between Slovakia and Hungary. The Slovaks replied that they treated their Hungarian minority better than the Hungarians treated their Slovak minority.

The fundamentalist response

Much like nationalism, religious fundamentalism has developed considerably over the last decade. Many countries are ripe for fundamentalism. It serves firstly to channel the need to find one's roots in an ever-changing world that is losing its landmarks, and secondly to nourish the desire to throw back the powerful invasion of "Western" and even Anglo-American culture. Muslim fundamentalism has gained a lot of ground since the early 1980s. The Shah had modernized and to an extent Westernized Iran, but the "revolution" of the fundamentalist Muslim mullahs made scrupulous religious observance obligatory: men and women were segregated, women had to cover themselves head-to-foot, a patriarchy was established. The American flag is regularly burned in bonfires in the streets of Teheran, while demonstrators shout their contempt for Western perversion. In much the same way, fundamentalists in Algeria, Egypt, Syria and Libya find in religion both a refuge and reasons to reject the West. As we have seen above, this rejection is illustrated for example by the assassination of foreigners in Egypt and Algeria and by bomb attacks on foreign buildings.

The response of decentralization

Closer to home, another response to the negative effects of globalization is the attempt to get back to the grassroots, whether in territorial communities, regions, cities or districts.

The following scene is in the United States. To get into a CID (Common Interest Development), you have to pass through a checkpoint at the gate. CIDs are not religious communities or bands of fanatics or criminals. Instead they are little cities governed by their own laws, within larger American cities. According to Prof. Evan McKenzie of the University of Illinois at Chicago, author of a bestseller on the subject: *"In the year 2000, 30 % of Americans will live concentrated in CIDs. That means the country will be segmented spatially in private territories that establish their own rules."* That 30 % figure may sound outlandish; actually, it reflects how widespread CIDs are becoming.

The co-owners of CIDs live in identical houses under the watchful gaze of video-cameras. If slow-moving and ineffective governments can't protect them, then they hope to protect themselves from the rise of violence and the perpetual changes brought on by globalization. They have their own policemen, whose role is to enforce strict CID rules covering garbage collection and disposal, sewage disposal, construction, highway clearing and maintenance, noise regulations, visits, the size of animals, the greeting of outsiders. CIDs have names like Placienta Lakes, Lake Wood Village and Boca Raton (Florida), Monroe (New Jersey) and Canyon Hill (California).

The anonymity and dehumanizing character of important world trends is leading some people to seek refuge in the region. Within the European Union, for example, the nation-state is in full retreat, since governmental powers are being transferred both upwards, from national capitals to Brussels, the capital of Europe, and downwards, to individual regions and cities. This movement is articulated in the principle of "subsidiarity," according to which powers are entrusted to the lowest level of government, the municipality. If a given problem cannot be solved at that level, then it is taken up further, first to the national level and subsquently to the level of the European community itself. The principle of subsidiarity is a kind of back-to-the-roots anti-globalization model. The assumption is that the government closest to the citizen is the municipal government. In the final analysis, this extreme form of decentralization is designed to give the citizens greater control over the situation.

Unfortunately, the model of decentralization runs headlong into the reality of global interdependence. By applying the principle of subsidiarity, it becomes clear that problems in many different areas can only be solved at a higher level. The back-to-the-roots approach may be gratifying, but the list of problems that can be solved locally is shrinking as global interdependence grows.

The continentalist response

The continentalist response is weakening the sovereignty of nation-states by seeking to create continent-sized, super-national power blocs. Two current examples of such continental blocs are NAFTA (the North American Free Trade Agreement) and the European Union.

NAFTA is a free-trade zone consisting for the moment of three countries: Canada, the United States and Mexico. Its objective is above all economic, since it is removing barriers to trade, natural resources and technology. Each member-state undertakes to reduce its powers in certain areas, in the interests of a free market.

The European Union is something else again, since its objective is political: the future creation of a federal or quasi-federal State, as laid out in the Treaty of Rome of 1957. The Europeans are using economic and social measures to arrive at that objective. Unlike NAFTA, the European Union is adopting the symbols of an enlarged nation-state: a European flag, a European anthem, a joint passport, a joint social charter, and eventually, a monetary union with a single currency, the "ecu."

The European Union model could be an alternative to globalization since it is transposing the expansion of markets from the planetary to the continental level, while transposing the concept of the nation-state from the level of countries to that of Europe as a whole. In other words, the European model is that of an emerging federal super-state, within which 390 million citizens in 15 countries can join forces to build their future and bring about their social project.

The globalist response: extend globalization instead of preventing it, by means of solutions to certain economic and social problems

We are the victims of the globalization of problems resulting from the rise of global interdependence. Unfortunately, there has been no corresponding movement toward the globalization of solutions. This asymmetry is creating serious and painful imbalances. Globalization without rules is creating a competitive context much like war without the Geneva Convention. The levelling effect of the lowest common denominator is leading to a dangerous dual economy, made up of the rich and the poor, of insiders and outsiders. The harmonization of social and environmental policies in the world would make it easier to solve the problems brought on by globalization, by establishing the same ground rules for all countries. In this respect, it would be possible to speak of a "GATT of Employment," in which the commercial agreements of the GATT would be extended; there could then be worldwide or regional minimum wages, and a social charter. (Valaskakis, 1994).

The Group of Lisbon, an international association, is carrying on the work of the celebrated Club of Rome, wants to improve the lot of humanity by means of concerted action. That is why the Group of Lisbon is proposing "world-contracts" that would open the way to a new culture of world cooperation and a "global" way of doing things.

Some people foresee the creation of a "world government," along confederal lines. This idea strikes us as hard to bring into being, because of the diversity of the world and the difficulty

31

of finding a mechanism of governance acceptable to one and all. The model "one person=one vote" could hardly constitute the basis of a world government, since it would give China, with its 1.2 billion inhabitants, a power that some countries would consider dangerous. The alternative model of "one dollar=one vote" would benefit rich countries and would likely accentuate inequality around the world. However, it might be plausible to progressively harmonize social policies at the world level, before moving on to the creation of a world government.

CONCLUSION

In the meantime, what should we do? This examination of the evolution of the planet and the new challenges facing us reveals a double dynamic at work: on the one hand are "centripetal" trends (favoring the central resolution of problems). On the other hand are "centrifugal" trends (favoring the decentralized and local resolution of these same problems).

The centripetal movement results from the rise of global interdependence (environment, security, geopolitics, Information Super Highway, etc.) and from the globalization of production, which itself is due to the emergence of an increasingly powerful political actor, the Stateless Corporation.

The centrifugal forces result from the attempts to create or strengthen nation-states, not to mention "tribal states," from the back-to-the-roots movement, and from religious fundamentalism that is hermetically closed to foreign influences.

European-style continentalization is an intermediary model having in our opinion a bright future, since it involves the harmonization of economic and social policies in the fifteen member-states. The European Union constitutes a new kind of federalism.

How does Quebec's independence movement relate to these broad world trends? It is a hybrid movement that finds certain principles of globalization and continentalization attractive (Quebec indépendantistes generally support NAFTA and the GATT), while seeking to make of Quebec an autonomous "little world" in control of its own destiny. This ambivalence is summed up in the mobilizing word - "sovereignty." Some people may aspire to this "sovereignty." Yet it remains an obscure concept, accessible only to specialists; it stems from contradictions, dreamlike illusions and a mistaken analysis of the situation in Canada. In the pages that follow, we will examine the contradictions contained in the idealized project of "sovereignty," by concentrating on the ten myths to be found at the root of the indépendantiste philosophy - ten myths that do not stand up to critical scrutiny. We invite readers to follow argument and counter-argument and to judge for themselves the validity of our ideas. We will place each of the myths in context, in order to explain its origin, after which we will study each myth point by point before drawing our conclusions.

PART ONE
The "sovereignist" sales pitch: ten enduring myths

Myth 1: Canadian federalism is rigid and unchanging

The context

Discussing the Constitution must be one of the favorite pastimes of Quebec's political elites. Even so, the debate on the future of Quebec's place in Canada has unfortunately been restricted to ready-made formulas, not to mention battles waged with statistics. "Federalism is the status quo," we often hear, "federalism cannot be reformed," "federalism costs Quebeckers a lot."

These slogans are tossed around so much, that they have turned the question of Quebec's fate into a nitpicking debate between experts, thereby excluding the majority of the population, who have understandably grown tired of the power struggles of specialists. Partisans of independence are trying to convince Quebeckers that since the Constitution cannot be reformed, Canadian federalism and Canada are a failure and there is no alternative to independence.

Ever since the Meech Lake and Charlottetown Accords were rejected, it has become common to hear that Canadian federalism is a rigid and unchanging system that creates political deadlocks and cannot be transformed. The indépendantistes are presenting Quebeckers with a misleading choice, expressed for example by the Bloc Québécois:

> *Quebeckers are facing a political choice that is simpler and clearer than ever before: the status quo or sovereignty. And an economic choice that is just as clear: stagnation or repatriating political powers to Quebec." (Programme du BQ, 1993:13).*

This enduring myth was already expressed in the Allaire Report (1991). After noting that in 1965 the Laurendeau-Dun-

37

ton Commission and in 1977 the Pépin-Robarts Commission already spoke of a "crisis," the Allaire Report asked:

Can a system of government remain in a perpetual state of crisis, without adjustments and changes being made to help it work better? Can the federal system be renewed? Is it still well-suited to its current and future setting?"

This mythology of a federalism both rigid and unchanging stems essentially from a poor understanding of the way federalism works and the purpose it serves, which is to recognize and accomodate differences. The mythology also takes as a point of departure a supposed triple equation: Constitution=federalism=Canada. In order to avoid this terminological confusion, however, it should be noted that constitutional changes are not the only means by which federalism evolves, and that Canada is more than just a federal system. In fact, as a country, Canada can influence the direction Canadian federalism takes.

Federalism is a system whose mission is the preservation of cultural and economic differences

The purpose of a federal structure is the preservation of social diversity, since federalism is above all a system that organizes powers in order to preserve differences. It reflects *"the desire expressed by certain groups to manage as they see fit the cultural and economic dimensions of their collective destiny."* (Dehousse, 1991:26).

As a result, the federal system plays a regulatory role: *"the object of a federal system is to stabilize political relationships in a community where lack of homogeneity makes it impossible to allow important questions to be settled by majority decision."* (Mallory, 1984:417).

A separation of powers resulting from the desire of autonomy means that each group, whether regional or cultural, controls the means by which to preserve and defend those characteristics distingishing it from other groups. Each country has its own history. That is why, when one looks at the more important federations around the the world, one is struck by how different they are: Australia, Canada, Belgium, the United States, Germany or even Switzerland. Depending on the country, the dividing-line between central (federal) jurisdictions and regional (provincial) jurisdictions is relatively stable or fluid.

In the United States, for example, the dividing line is much more fluid than in Canada, and federal jurisdictions south of the border have expanded, making the American federal system more centralized. In Canada, the respective jurisdictions of the central and provincial governments are much more clearly-defined, even in the case of shared jurisdictions and federal-provincial coordinating mechanisms (which are separate from exclusive jurisdictions). The importance attributed to this distribution of powers is part of the interpration that the jursiprudence has made of the British North America Act (1867). One has only to recall the position defended by Lord Atkin in 1937 (A.G. for Canada v. A.G. for Ontario [1937] A.C. 326, p.351), when he said that the distribution of powers between the Dominion and its provinces was the most important condition allowing the Act to bring about the inter-provincial pact.

Canada's federation is essentially asymmetrical

In Canada, this rather sharp delineation between provincial and federal jurisdictions reflects the asymmetrical character of the Canadian federation, which is made up of provinces whose demographic and economic weight and ethno-cultural makeup are distinct.

That is why provinces have practically exclusive control in all those domains where societies like Quebec can preserve their distinctiveness: culture, education, local administration, civil law. Moreover, the Canadian federal system has continually evolved since its creation, in order to adapt to new circumstances and to respect the principle of distinctiveness.

This "asymmetry" creates some tensions between common values and the desire to preserve autonomy. In Canada, those tensions are twofold. The first kind of tension shows up in federal-provincial relations, since the essence of the federal system is that each government seeks to increase its political powers: the federal government places emphasis on national interests, where provincial governments defend the interests of their region, sometimes to the detriment of national interests. These tensions may sometimes strike the citizens as irritating not to mention worrisome, because of the way the media cover them. One has only to remember the way Alberta threatened to cut off the rest of Canada's energy supply in the early 1980s, in order to protest against the National Energy Program. The fact there are such frictions is ample proof that the central government does not dominate provincial governments, which enjoy a great deal of autonomy.

The minority situation of Quebec, which has developed as a distinct society, and of French Canadians in Canada generally, is another source of tension.

Quebec is distinct both as a province and because of the fact a majority French-speaking cultural community is rooted in Quebec. Its minority status within North America has forced it to keep careful watch over the precise separation of powers at every level. That in turn is judged indispensable for keeping Quebec "distinct" and explains why, since 1960, it has sought greater legislative powers.

As a result, any possible federal interference has always been seen, not as a move to serve common interests, but as an instrument of domination.

While it is doubtless true that Canada's constitutional history has been shaped by the desire for autonomy of both the provinces and the francophone minority, history is not made up solely of conflicts that were never resolved! Quite the contrary.

By respecting the distinctiveness of Quebec, Canadian federalism has evolved "along with" Canada rather than "in spite of" Canada. It is not just the institutions that have put their imprint on the country, but also society itself that has given a particular form to the institutions.

Quebec often sees itself as a fortress forced to defend itself from the onslaught of "English" federal power. This image is compelling, but is nonetheless false. Certainly, French Canadians have refused to be assimilated and Quebec has peacefully taken up the same struggle. But the affirmation of the French fact in Canada has been possible because the philosophy of Canada was open to cultural differences.

Canada is not just a federal system that organizes power-sharing. It is a country with a territory, values, economic, social and cultural links, a federal political system, a system of laws, roads, people, provinces, houses.

As a country, Canada has had to find ways to respond to the challenge of accomodating differences and dealing with cultural and economic asymmetry. Since the federal system is capable of evolving, economic and cultural differences have been respected, and the country has been able to adapt both to internal and external changes in the modern world. Canadian responses to diversity have been legal, legislative and constitutional. A good example is the Canadian invention of transfer payments, according to which the wealthier provinces pay for the poorer ones. We will see later on that this is a response to the economic disparity of the provinces and has significantly benefitted Quebec. We will also see that the cultural distinctiveness of a province like Quebec is not only able to develop within the federal system - this distinctiveness is backed up in many ways at the Canadian level, by such measures as the Official Languages Act as well as the financing of Radio-Canada (the French service of the Canadian Broadcasting Corporation), the Office National du Film (the French service of the National Film Board) and the Canada Council....

Canadian federalism is a dynamic and constantly-evolving system, quite apart from constitutional reform

We have already seen that the attribution of exclusive areas of jurisdiction to the provinces was one of the ways to preserve differences within this asymmetric federation.

But the division of powers does not tell the whole story. In fact, the federal system has not just evolved by means of constitutional amendments.

According to Senator Gérald-A. Beaudoin, an expert on constitutional law:

Canadian federalism has never stopped evolving over the years... and continues to evolve even without constitutional amendments." (Beaudoin, 1994 a:B-3).

Indeed, the failure to revise the 1982 Constitution after the Meech Lake and Charlottetown Accords were rejected is not as serious as some people would like us to think. We were so often told that the changes outlined in these accords were vital for our future as Quebeckers that we started to believe that. But we forgot at the same time that Quebec was part of a country, Canada, that encouraged it to be different.

Besides constitutional amendments, Canada has five other tools for changing the federal system: court judgments; frequent constitutional conferences; interprovincial conferences inaugurated by Honoré Mercier in 1887 and taken up again by Jean Lesage in 1960; the reports of parliamentary committees and Royal Commissions on the subject of the Constitution; administrative agreements that help federalism adapt to a changing environment (Beaudoin, 1994a:B-3).

The special importance for Quebec of administrative agreements should be noted. The federal government has managed the family-allowance program across Canada since 1945. But since 1974, an administrative agreement with Ottawa has enabled Quebec to distribute the family-allowance envelope in line with the particular needs of Quebec's policy favoring more births.

At the same time, Quebec has run its own pension plan since 1966, while other provinces have delegated the job to the federal government. And since the Cullen-Couture agreement came into effect in 1978, Quebec has had a say in the selection of immigrants, on the basis of a joint agreement, according to criteria established by the governments both of Canada and of Quebec.

We do not intend to give a course on constitutional law. It is enough to say that the history of Canadian federalism has been marked by important, broad changes and an ability to adapt to new circumstances (Beaudoin, 1994a:B-3). The original, rather centralized federal system adopted in 1867 has given way to a more decentralized system, thanks to the work of the Judicial Committee of the Privy Council, which has broadened the powers of the provinces while restricting those of the federal government. In times of conflict, during the First and Second World Wars, the system temporarily became more centralized. But then significant changes came about: unemployment insurance (1949); old-age pensions and additional benefits (1964). Starting in 1950, federal-provincial constitutional conferences have played a big role in shaping federalism: the federal spending power was recognized, on the basis of a 1937 decision by the Privy Council, the principle of transfer payments was clarified (and was articulated in Section 36 of the 1982 Constitution). More recently, interprovincial trade barriers were eliminated (July 1994) and the infrastructure program was set up (1993).

Federal-provincial diplomacy has been a tool of adaptation and change

Quite apart from the major governmental decisions that the public hears of, there also exists a sort of "federal-provincial diplomacy" in the Canadian federal system (Malory, 1984), of cooperation between the different levels of government. This cooperation has become indispensable because the different levels of government in the modern world are interdependent.

Canadian federalism has had to adjust to that reality over the years.

This federal-provincial diplomacy, Prof. Mallory notes,

"made possible solutions to problems created by the need to fit modern demands on the State into a constitutional framework designed in the very different conditions of the nineteenth century." (Mallory, 1984:446).

That is the reason firstly for federal-provincial conferences (bringing together the Prime Minister of Canada, the provincial Premiers, the ministers of intergovernmental affairs and their advisers), and secondly for regular meetings of ministers covering particular subjects.

During these meetings questions as varied as constitutional amendments, tax sharing and cost-shared programs are thrashed out.

Agreements are often concluded and submitted for ratification to the national Parliament and provincial assemblies.

By 1988 and 1992, the federal and Quebec governments reached no less than 244 administrative agreements (Privy Council, 1992).

Excellent results can be obtained by means of intergovernmental cooperation, since it avoids the frustration of debating constitutional amendments.

CONCLUSION

In the debate on reforming Canadian federalism, people often forget that Canada is much more than the federal system alone. Federalism is a system that organizes powers and is only one component of the country. The system reflects the desire of certain groups of society to manage as they see fit the cultural and economic dimensions of their collective destiny. From this desire proceeds a distribution of powers between the centre and the regions called federalism. It varies from one country to the next.

44

In Canada, the federation is asymmetrical, since it is made up of different provinces with different demographic and economic characteristics, as well as two "founding" linguistic communities, the anglophones and the francophones, not to mention the native people. From this asymmetry has grown a quite clear distribution of powers, assigning some jurisdictions to the federal government and others to the provinces and still others to both levels of government. This organization can lead to centrifugal pressures on the federal system, because of provincial desires to defend jurisdictions and because of the francophone-anglophone duality, which is why Quebec keeps such a close watch over its position.

Canada has offered very original and innovative responses to this double desire for autonomy. On the one hand, thanks to the pragmatic nature of its federalism, Canada accords a large amount of cultural and economic autonomy to those provinces, like Quebec, that desire it. And the system is continually evolving, even without constitutional amendments, essentially by means of "federal-provincial diplomacy," which leads to many agreements. On the other hand, the Canadian federal Parliament has recognized the cultural and economic diversity of Canada, by such measures as the Official Languages Act and the system of transfer payments, which allows for a more equitable sharing of wealth among the provinces.

On the eve of the 21st century, at a time when countries all over the world are joining together, Canada has already found in federalism a first response to the challenge of economic and cultural diversity. The system is constantly evolving. Why seek to separate Quebec from the rest of Canada? Why withdraw from federalism, when the federal system is designed to preserve differences and has proven to be both flexible and adaptable, even without constitutional amendments?

Myth 2:
THE CANADIAN FEDERAL STATE
IS TOO CENTRALIZED

The context

Some indépendantistes say that Canada is such a centralized federation that Quebec is being literally smothered under the federal yoke. An objective comparison of modern federal states leads us to conclude, however, that the Canadian federation is probably the most decentralized in the world. It is by far the most decentralized member of NAFTA, the trade bloc that also comprises the United States and Mexico. While Mexico is officially a federal state, the concentration of power there makes it a unitary state for all practical purposes. In the United States, the federation is highly centralized. The capital, Washington, is located in a federal district outside of the jurisdiction of the fifty states. In Canada, the national capital straddles the Ontario-Quebec border and there is no federal district. As for other federations in the world, such as Germany, Australia and Argentina, they are far more centralized than Canada. The Swiss federal republic alone can be compared to Canada, when it comes to decentralization. To dispel the unfounded myth of overly-centralized power in Canada, we invite the reader to compare Canada, the United States and Switzerland.

CANADA VS. THE UNITED STATES: WHICH IS MORE DECENTRALIZED?

When the comparison is made between the two federations, three important differences show up:

First difference: Canadian provinces are "sovereign" in some areas while American states are without real powers

The development of the two federations has followed two completely opposite paths. The Canadian federation has undergone change from the very beginning. Canada was originally centralized, but has become progressively decentralized, as we have seen above. Indeed, the central authority has weakened, as a result of practice and judicial decisions, favoring the provinces, whose powers have progressively grown between 1867 and 1994. Canada adopted a British-style parliamentary system (see the Statute of Westminster of 1931) and repatriated its Constitution in 1981.

In the United States, meanwhile, the text of the American Constitution calls for a very decentralized system, in which the states and the central government work in close cooperation. But progressively, practice and judicial decisions have led to a centralization of power in the hands of the executive and legislative branches of the government, to the detriment of the fifty states. The President of the United States is elected according to the principle of indirect universal suffrage. Even if the president does not have control over legislative power, he is nonetheless the formal and respected head of state of all Americans.

Little by little, the American government has centralized power by using the *"interstate commerce clause."* The interpretation of this clause has turned it into the most important limit imposed by the Constitution on the exercise of power by the fifty states.

Article 1 paragraph 3 of the Constitution of the United States says that the Congress has the power *"to regulate commerce with foreign nations, and among the several states, and with the Indian tribes."* With the passage of time, "commerce" under federal jurisdiction has come to be interpreted as including non-commercial acts:

"Today, 'commerce' in the constitutional sense, and hence 'interstate commerce,' covers every species of movement of persons and things, whether for profit or not, across state lines, every species of communication, every species of transmission of intelligence, whether for commercial purposes or otherwise, every species of commercial negotia-

tion which will involve sooner or later an act of transpor-
tation of persons or things, or the flow of services or power,
across state lines." (Congress, 1987).

This clause, interpreted in such broad terms, considerably limits the power of the fifty states.

Americans have long believed that the existence of a centralized American federation, with powers concentrated at the centre, helped preserve the unity of the country. That is why, in the 1860s, the central authority rejected the demands of the South, which wanted the sharing of jurisdictions to be decentralized. And when the decentralized South sought to preserve its right to maintain the institution of slavery, the Civil War, or War of Secession, broke out. The North, meanwhile, wanted a strong central State, and pushed for the creation of a highly centralized federation.

The American federation was subsequently strengthened by the progressive introduction of a "melting pot" culture, which encouraged the assimilation of immigrants into American society. This culture is characterized by the adoption of American national values, voluntary and sometimes obligatory renunciation of any other citizenship, learning English - which has become virtually the sole language of communication in the home, and the adoption by many immigrants of shorter surnames that are easier to pronounce. These values have contributed to the creation of a nation-wide spirit in America, which has become the "trademark" of American culture, and is devoted to the pursuit of happiness, freedom of expression and economic prosperity.

As we will see later on, the states of the Union are now demanding changes. Mike Leavitt, the Governor of Utah, recently said: "States are not merely lobbyists or a special interest group. States are co-equal players in the federal system and this process reasserts their proper role." (Fournier, 1995)

For its part, the Canadian federation has moved in the opposite direction. Throughout its history, Canada has constantly tried to strike a balance between centralizing pressures (such as national policies at the end of the nineteenth century and the National Energy Program of 1980) and decentralizing pressures (such as the Charlottetown Accord). In general, as we saw earlier on in the analysis of Myth 1, the constitutional history of Canada has beEn characterized by a progressive decentralization of the federation, as a way of responding to the demands of the country's cultural and economic asymmetry.

Consequently, in political terms, Canada presents several distinguishing features: the ten provinces are sovereign in some fields of jurisdiction, such as education. Moreover, federal ministers treat their provincial counterparts on an equal footing, which sometimes slows down the decision-making process. But that equal treatment has the advantage of allowing both for consultation and for the respect of fields of jurisdiction. Federal-provincial constitutional conferences are held for the purpose of reaching agreements. Although the Prime Minister of Canada presides over the conferences, he has no veto power. As a result, the provinces can reach their own decisions on areas under their authority, even if the Prime Minister doesn't agree.

Second difference: Canadian provincial premiers have more power than their American opposite numbers

When the Canadian Prime Minister has a majority in the House of Commons, he or she can be said to have more power than a President of the United States with a minority in the Congress. Even so, the President of the United States, elected by a college of electors (who in turn are elected on the basis of universal suffrage), is the head of state, whatever happens, and the respected spokesman of all Americans. Moreover, the president has a veto power over all legislation voted by the Congress, which can overturn the presidential veto with a two-thirds vote (article 1-7 of the Constitution of the United States of America). In addition, the President of the United States cannot be removed from office during his mandate, unless he is subjected to the cumbersome and grave procedure of "impeachment."

But above all, the central American government, taken as a whole, has far more power than the central Canadian government, since the governors of American states have less room for manoeuvre than Canadian provincial premiers. The premiers can, for example, oppose certain federal initiatives, whether individually or together with their opposite numbers from other provinces.

It would be hard to imagine such a situation in the United States, or to imagine American states enjoying the same amount of freedom as Quebec or Ontario have to act on the international scene. These latter two provinces have general delegations in the countries of their choice and their delegates sometimes act independently of Canadian diplomats. This example is significant, since it illustrates just how decentralized the Canadian system really is.

During the negotiations leading to the Free Trade Agreement and the North American Free Trade Agreement, the premiers of Canadian provinces (or their representatives) were regularly consulted by the federal government. Some dispositions of NAFTA provide specifically for the protection of some provincial trade practices, while in other cases the provinces accepted that NAFTA change their established practices. Without such close collaboration, the treaty would not have had much real value.

The American states were not as closely involved in the negotiations, since they have very limited authority. As we have already seen above, the *"interstate commerce clause"* establishes interstate and international commerce as a federal jurisdiction.

At the same time, all Canadian provinces were present and directly involved in negotiations at the Uruguay Round of the GATT (which entered into effect on January 1, 1995).

And when Prime Minister Jean Chrétien visited China, he went at the head of Team Canada, which was made up of 300 businessmen and the premiers of each province, with the exception of Jacques Parizeau who claimed to be too busy to go. Could we imagine such a situation in the United States? The President has sometimes been accompanied by a state governor or two during trips abroad to make pitches for trade, but never by the governors of all fifty states.

Third difference: the central American government is much stronger than the central Canadian government

Clearly, the central authority in the United States is much stronger. A comparison of the Canadian and American systems of government shows that in Canada the provinces have far broader powers than the fifty American states.

In Canada, the federal government does not directly respresent the interests of the provinces at the legislative level. The Canadian Senate, on the model of the British House of Lords, is made up of people appointed by the Prime Minister. This situation requires the Prime Minister to carry on regular consultations with the provincial premiers. The provincial premiers and ministers are consulted by their federal opposite numbers, on an equal footing. Moreover, the provinces are sovereign in some fields of exclusive jurisdiction.

In the United States, the interests of the fifty states are directly represented within the central government by senators, who are elected on the basis of universal suffrage. As a result, the central government acts in the direct interests of the American people, through the House of Representative and the Houses of individual states, as well as through the Senate, which has two Senators per state. And as we have seen already, the Congress profits handsomely from the elastic interpretation that is made of the *"interstate commerce clause."*

Consequently, much to the dismay of American states, the Congress is in a position to pass laws of national scope, which are useless for some states and extremely costly to apply. It has been estimated that applying various national environmental laws, such as the "Clean Air Act" and the "Clean Waters Act" would cost $44 billion. The Senate has just tabled a bill, requiring the Congress to provide the states with budgetary allocations whenever it passes national laws that have financial implications (*New York Times,* January 6, 1995).

The dominating character of the central American government can lead to signficiant tensions. For example, some American states want to create a "Conference of the states," in order to fight what they consider to be a growing imbalance between the respective powers of the federal government and the state governments. The states see their room for manoeuvre dwindling, and complain that Washington is imposing both good and bad laws on them, without consultation and without worrying whether the states have the financial capacity to apply the laws.

If the idea of a Conference of the states is accepted by the majority of state Congresses, the conference will meet in Fall 1995. It will determine what is the best way to redress the imbalance of powers, and will make recommendations that will then be presented to the Congress. Everyone agrees a national debate is needed on the balance of powers. Tom Ridge, Governor of Pennsylvania, recently told the *Wall Street Journal* (January 3, 1995): "I served in Congress for 12 years, and we trod on the rights of states every day. That will change only when they speak with a national voice."

But even if a new balance of powers is negotiated by the states and the central government, the federal system will remain far more centralized in the United States than in Canada.

THE CANADA-SWITZERLAND COMPARISON

Switzerland is said to be the most decentralized federation in the industrial world, with Canada in second-place. The indépendantistes often cite the example of Switzerland as a model of decentralization. That is why we have chosen to compare Canada to Switzerland.

To compare the degree of decentralization of the Canadian and Swiss federations, which could be considered the two world finalists in this category, we will use two indicators:

- the more a federation is decentralized, the more provinces will have exclusive jurisdictions.

- the more a federation is centralized, the more the federal State will have exclusive jurisdictions.

With regard to the degree of financial decentralization, we will use two more indicators:

- the more a federation is decentralized, the more the provinces will have their own sources of revenue to fulfil their constitutional responsibilities.

- once again, the more a federation is decentralized, the more the provinces will be able to freely spend their revenues without spending constraints being imposed by the federal government.

It will be noted that the rise of the welfare state since the Second World War has broadened and made more complex the fields of activity of the different levels of government, making it necessary that the two levels of government cooperate more closely. As a result, it is increasingly difficult to distinguish clearly which level is at work since the levels of government cooperate closely to provide government services and assume part of the financial costs. Some authors speak of "interconnected federalisms" to describe this new financial interdependence within federal states.

Let us look at a few points of comparison between Switzerland and Canada:

Exclusive provincial jurisdictions:

In Canada, the two levels of government are bound by the Constitution. That is why the Supreme Court of Canada ensures that each level of government respect the jursidictions of the other level. If a federal law is in conflict with a provincial law, in what the Constitution recognizes as an area under provincial authority, then the provincial law will prevail. Canadian provinces are really sovereign in their fields of jurisdiction.

In Switzerland, cantonal laws, even those falling under cantonal jurisdiction, can be stricken down by the Supreme Court if they enter into conflict with federal laws.

Exclusive federal jurisdictions

Canadian provinces are able to act exclusively or pre-eminently in more fields of jurisdiction than Swiss cantons (9 in Canada compared to 4 in Switzerland for the Swiss government, see Table 1). Indeed, the Swiss government has exclusive jurisdictions in more areas than the central government in Canada (19 for Switzerland as against 13 for Canada, see Table 2). Besides, it is interesting to note that the central Swiss government has exclusive jurisdiction in 5 areas which are areas of shared federal-provincial jurisdiction in Canada. These areas are: immigration, labor, the environment, agriculture and natural resources (see Tables 2 and 3).

The degree of financial autonomy of the provinces

Canadian provinces have much more financial autonomy than Swiss cantons. The degree of financial autonomy in a federal state can be assessed using two indicators: first, the share of the provinces in total receipts of the public sector, and second, the share of the provinces in the expenses of the public sector.

The Canadian and Swiss federal governments have about the same percentage of total receipts: 49 % in the case of Canada, ad 50 % in the case of Switzerland. But there is a marked difference between Canadian provinces, which have

41 % of total receipts, and Swiss cantons, which have 28 % (see Table 4).

Regarding expenses, the central Swiss government spends a slightly higher proportion of the total (48 %) than the Canadian federal government (43.6 %). But the provinces make 40.6 % of total expenses, compared to the 30 % share in expenses of the Swiss cantons. It is important to bear in mind that intergovernmental transfers represent a significant portion of the expenses of the Canadian federal govenrment (see Table 5).

Autonomy with respect to transfer payments

In Switzerland and in Canada, as in other federal states, there are two types of intergovernmental transfers: unconditional transfers and conditional transfers. In both countries, unconditional transfers are generally transfer payments made by the federal state to the provinces (or cantons). These payments are designed to reduce the fiscal gap between wealthier and less-wealthy provinces, so that less-wealthy provinces needn't resort to additional taxes in order to provide same basic public services that wealthier provinces can offer. No condition is attached to the way these transfers are used. Conditional transfers are also payments made by the federal state. But they are designed to cover the costs of specific programs which the federal government designates as programs of national importance. In both countries, these payments are designed to fund vast social programs which fall under the constitutional jurisdiction of the provinces (or cantons).

In most federal states, conditional transfers are accompanied by specific conditions on the way in which the provinces may dispose of these funds. If the provinces do not maintain the national standards upheld by the federal government, then the provinces will not receive the transfers. This is a way for the central government to influence the decision-making process of the provinces, when transfers represent a large portion of their total receipts. Since the provinces depend on federal subsidies, they are required to respect federal directives to avoid raising their own taxes - an unpopular measure which could cost them votes at election time. This kind of transfer induces the provinces to make their political choices in accordance with federal objectives.

But the restrictive aspect of these transfers depends on the controls exercised by the federal government on the provinces. Just how tight the controls are varies widely from one country to another. The federal government may choose not to use any of the following measures: approving plans, imposing rules and procedures, getting federal managers involved in the administration of programs, inspections and on-site accounting controls, etc.

In this respect, Canada is more decentralized than Switzerland, since the provinces receive less conditional transfers from the federal government than the Swiss cantons do (64 % in Canada, compared to 70 % in Switzerland, see Table 6). In Switzerland, the formal percentages reflect the real nature of conditional transfers, since the Swiss federal republic exercises tight control over the use cantons make of conditional transfers (Orban, 1984:331). That is not the case in Canada.

In Canada, conditional transfers are called "specific purpose transfers." These payments are designed to support certain clearly-defined social programs and are in line with the definition of conditional transfers. However, in the vast majority of cases, the Canadian government does not exercise any control over the use of these funds, practising instead an "arm's-length" policy. As a result, some so-called "conditional" transfers turn into "unconditional" transfers, since provinces can spend them as they see fit.

In Canada, conditional transfers over which the federal government exercises tight control only amount to 18.4 % of total transfers (see Table 6), which makes Canada a considerably more decentralized federation than Switzerland, where "conditional" transfers amount to 70 % of total transfers (Smiley, 1984: 42). Given the largely unconditional nature of Canadian federal transfers, we can see that the provinces spend as they see fit about two-thirds (66 %) of all expenses of the public sector in Canada, while the cantons are only able to spend 30 % of total public-sector expenses in Switzerland as they see fit. (Mallory, 1984: 413).

CONCLUSION

Canada wins the gold medal for decentralization!

The supposedly excessive centralization of the Canadian federal State, forever invading fields of provincial jurisdiction, is simply an invention with no concrete basis in fact. It is true that there are some areas where the two levels of government act jointly. This can be attributed to the fact that the Fathers of Confederation could not foresee the emergence of all the areas where states intervene nowadays (environmental protection, manpower training, research and development, industrial strategies, etc.) According to the original plan of 1867, power-sharing was approximate and kept to a minimum. The evolution of society since then has served to make the problem of power-sharing more complex, not only in Canada but around the world. But if one takes the trouble to examine objective facts instead of sticking to arbitrary doctrines and emotional slogans, one will come to the well-documented conclusion that no federation in the world, not even Switzerland, is more decentralized than our own.

Some people may object that Swiss decentralization is to be found most of all at the level of the citizens, who, by virtue of article 89 of the constitution, have the right to a referendum on federal laws and orders of a general nature that have been voted on by the federal assembly (as long as 50,000 active citizens or eight cantons have requested the referendum). Some might conclude from this example that Switzerland is more decentralized than Canada. That would only mean that Canada is the second-most-decentralized federation in the industrial world!

Consequently, it would not be appropriate to call for a still greater dilution of the federal State, whether by means of the sort of sovereignty-association some people dream of in Quebec, or massive decentralization such as is proposed by some regional parties in Western Canada. Such measures would hinder the much-required integrated management of interdependence.

In fact, one of the driving forces of Quebec separatism is the absence of centralization in Canada. Premier Jacques Parizeau and Vice-Premier Bernard Landry have publicly said several times that they became indépendantistes because Canada was too weak. The theory that Canada is excessively centralized should therefore be scrapped, since it is totally without foundation.

If one adds to constitutional analysis an analysis of the balance of economic powers between the central government and regional governments, it is clear that the American government is much more powerful than the Canadian federal government. The American government is the real boss, because of its regulatory and legislative power as well as its spending power. It would be hard to imagine the governor of the state of New York or of California contradicting the economic policies of the American government, or defying its authority. In Canada, meanwhile, large provinces like Ontario and Quebec can have macro-economic policies that contradict those of the federal government. Moreover, the spending power of the provinces as a whole is greater than that of the federal government. The federal government's share in the total budget of the Canadian public sector is now less than 40 %, the rest being in the hands of the provincial governments.

TABLE 1
EXCLUSIVE PROVINCIAL JURISDICTIONS

CANADA	SWITZERLAND
1. Education	1. Primary and secondary education
2. Administration of justice	2. Administration of justice
3. Social welfare	3. Social welfare
4. Post-secondary education	4. Language
5. Manpower training	
6. Forests	
7. Property	
8. Health*	
9. Civi Law	

Sources: (Kloti, 1988:94; Hughes, 1982:3-80; Rémillard, 1980: 604-606; Beaudoin, 1982).
* To simplify comparisons, we have not been able to use the exact terms of the Constitution.

TABLE 2
EXCLUSIVE FEDERAL JURISDICTIONS

CANADA	SWITZERLAND
1. Postal service	1. Postal service
2. Armed Forces	2. Armed Forces
3. Foreign Policy	3. Foreign Policy
4. Customs	4. Customs
5. Navigation	5. Navigation
6. Banks and Mint	6. Banks and Mint
7. Criminal Law	7. Criminal Law
8. Divorce	8. Divorce
9. Railways	9. Railways
10. Telegraphs	10. Telegraphs
11. Weights and measures	11. Weights and measures
12. Unemployment insurance	12. Unemployment insurance
13. Citizenship	13. Citizenship
	14. Immigration
	15. Manpower training
	16. Agriculture
	17. Civil Code
	18. Labor Relations
	19. Natural resources

Sources: (Kloti, 1988:94; Hughes, 1982:3-80; Rémillard, 1980: 604-606; Beaudoin, 1982).

60

TABLE 3
SHARED JURISDICTIONS

CANADA	SWITZERLAND
1. Culture	1. Culture
2. Road transportation	2. Road transportation
3. Industry and commerce	3. Industry and commerce
4. Language	4. Forests
5. Police	5. Health
6. Immigration	6. Post-secondary education
7. Labor relations	7. Property
8. Environment	
9. Agriculture	
10. Natural resources	

Sources: (Kloti, 1988:94; Hughes, 1982:3-80; Rémillard, 1980: 604-606; Beaudoin, 1982).

TABLE 4
TOTAL REVENUE

CANADA (1989)		SWITZERLAND (1989)*	
Federal	49 %	Federal	50 %
Provinces	41 %	Cantons	28 %
Municipal	10 %	Municipal	22 %
TOTAL	100 %	TOTAL	100 %

Source: (Government Finance Statistics, 1993: 170-176, 514-518; Annuaire statistique de la Suisse, 1994).
* The percentages forSwitzerland represent estimates based on data provided by Government Finance Statistics.

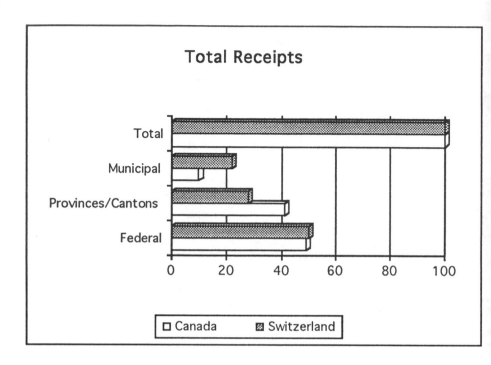

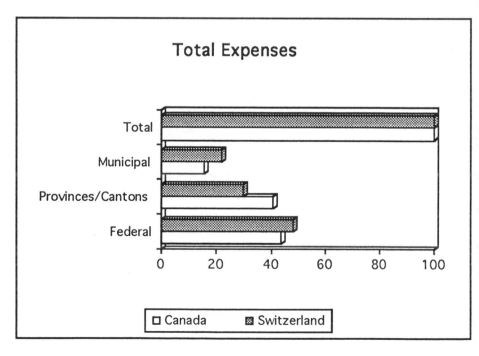

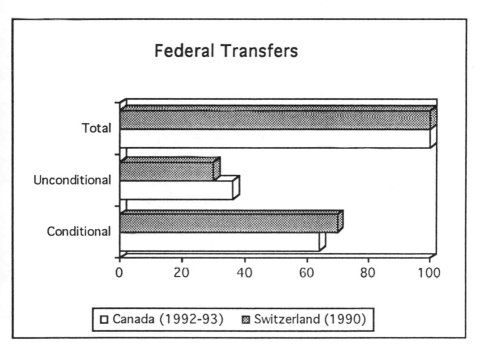

TABLE 5
TOTAL SPENDING

CANADA (1989)		SWITZERLAND (1989)*	
Federal	43,6 %	Federal	48 %
Provinces	40,6 %	Cantons	30 %
Municipal	15,8 %	Municipal	22 %
TOTAL	100 %	TOTAL	100 %

Source: (Government Finance Statistics, 1993: 170-176, 514-518; Annuaire statistique de la Suisse, 1994).
* The percentages forSwitzerland represent estimates based on data provided by Government Finance Statistics and l'Annuaire statistique de la Suisse, 1994.

TABLE 6
FEDERAL TRANSFERS

CANADA (1992-93)		SWITZERLAND (1990)**	
Conditional	64 % (18,4 %)*	Conditional	70 %
Unconditional	36 % (81,6 %)	Unconditional	30 %
TOTAL	100% (100%)	TOTAL	100 %

Sources: (Annuaire du Canada, 1994; Bird, 1986:46; Smiley, 1984:42; Annuaire statistique de la Suisse, 1994).
* The figures in parentheses represent estimates of the real distinction between consitional and unconditional tranfsers once the federal government's lack of control over so-called 'conditional' tranfers to the provinces is taken into account. (Smiley, 1984:46).
**Estimates based on l'Annuaire statistique de la Suisse (1994) et Bird (1986)

Myth 3:
Federalism costs Quebeckers a lot

"Statistics are innocent and only confess under torture"
(popular saying)

Context

A week hardly goes by without someone saying that the constitutional status quo is unacceptable. Seperation is the answer for some people, while others advocate constitutional reform.

Indépendantistes assure us that federalism costs Quebeckers a lot, and that independence, by putting an end to duplication and overlaps, would result in substantial savings. They add that it is time to abandon the rudderless ship called Canada, because nothing on board works anymore: the failure of the Meech Lake and Charlottetown Accords is ample proof that federalism cannot be reformed. For a public well aware of the need to clean up public finances, the Parti Québécois proposes a single remedy: sovereignty. On page 63 of its 1994 program, the PQ tells us that *"sovereignty will bring about substantial savings thanks to the rationalization of public expenses, once the operations of the two levels of government are merged. A reduction of the administrative costs of government operations would result in savings of from two to three billion dollars."* (Parti Québécois, 1994:63).

Quebec's minister of Restructuring, Richard Le Hir, told the newspaper *La Presse* on November 2, 1994 that the Quebec government would save substantial sums after independence, by eliminating government overlaps and duplication (Fontaine, 1994: B-4). He was sharply criticized by experts for issuing a highly questionable set of figures supposedly backing up his case (November 14 and 15, 1994).

In the same vein, the Bloc Québécois states in its program that:

65

"a sovereign Quebec will be better able to manage healthy public finances, a high priority at the moment ... [since] the countless overlaps of jurisdiction between Quebec and Ottawa will be eliminated, as well as the waste they cause." (Bloc Québécois, 1993: 70).

This position implies that belonging to a federation is only worthwhile as long as a province gets at least as much money out of the federation as it puts in, by way of taxes.

Such an approach is misleading, however, since there is far more to Canadian federalism than columns of statistics. Indeed, federalism offers the possibility of achieving greater things together. It is highly simplistic to limit the debate about Quebec's part in Canada to some kind of federal-provincial balance sheet. By being a part of Canada, Quebec can not only accomplish more at a lesser cost, but can also accomplish things it couldn't do alone. Pooling our social, cultural, economic, financial and institutional strengths with the rest of the country creates synergies in many areas. Being part of Canada means sharing a territory, a passport, an economic union, a monetary union, a project of social justice (social programs); it means being open to culture (two languages)... It also means being able to develop a social project. Being part of Canada has many advantages, not all of which can be measured in statistics.

We have placed in context the myth that federalism costs Quebeckers a lot. We will now explore the two parts of this myth, neither of which is well-founded.

- First part of the myth: Canadian federalism costs Quebeckers a lot, since Quebec receives less than its "fair share."

- Second part of the myth: Canadian federalism costs a lot because of government overlaps and duplication, and independence would result in significant savings.

FIRST PART OF THE MYTH: FEDERALISM COSTS QUEBECKERS A LOT, SINCE QUEBEC GETS LESS THAN ITS "FAIR SHARE"

What they tell us: "Federalism costs Quebeckers a lot, and Quebec does not get its 'fair share' of federal spending."

The reality: Quebec profits from being part of the federation.

The Parti Québécois and the Bloc Québécois have often said that Quebeckers do not receive their "fair share" of what Ottawa distributes to the provinces. People find this idea shocking, since it gives them the impression that Quebec is a "poor cousin," always served last and always getting less than the others (and particularly less than Ontario). Some Quebeckers conclude that they get less back from the federal government than they pay out in the form of taxes.

While recognizing the limits both of statistical comparisons and of the notion of "a fair share," we will show that the figures do not support the view that Quebec is exploited. In fact, Quebec benefits handsomely from the Canadian economic union, and receives from the federal government a larger share than either its share of the Canadian population or of Canada's gross domestic product would justify. Indeed, Quebec receives more than the other provinces and for the last few decades has got more back from the federal government than it has paid out.

For the last few decades, Quebec has got more back from the federal government than it has paid out in the form of taxes.

It may seem difficult to navigate through statistics that do not always agree. One conclusion is inescapable however: Quebec has benefitted handsomely from the federal system.

Since 1972, Quebec has received an average of $2.3 billion per year more than it has paid to Ottawa. According to a 1990 study undertaken by André Raynauld for the Conseil du patronat du Québec (Quebec Employers Council), if Quebec had separated in 1980, it would have lost between $23 billion and

$27 billion. For the period 1980 to 1988, these figures do not include debt-service costs. For 1986 alone, the shortfall would have resulted in tax increases corresponding to 1.5 % of Quebec's GDP and around 3.5 % of all taxes collected in Quebec (Raynauld, 1990:17).

According to the same study, in 1988 Quebec paid less federal taxes (23 %) than its share of revenue or of Canada's gross domestic product (24 %). As for federal spending in Quebec, it was equivalent to 24 % of all federal spending across Canada, a share corresponding to Quebec's share of Canada's gross domestic product.

This spending can be broken down into three categories. First of all, spending on goods and services - something on which indépendantistes like to focus narrowly, since Quebec only receives 18 % of the Canadian total in this category. Then transfers to individuals (pensions, unemployment insurance benefits, etc.) which rise to 24 % of the total. And finally, intergovernmental transfers - here Quebec got 32 % of the Canadian total, or much more than its 24 % share of the gross domestic product or 23 % share of taxes paid. In 1988, meanwhile, Ontario represented 41.2 % of Canada's gross domestic product, and taxes paid by Ontario taxpayers represented 45 % of all fiscal receipts of the federal government. But federal spending in Ontario only amounted to 28 % of all spending in Canada.

In 1988, Quebec registered a net fiscal gain of from $800 million to $1 billion, because of fiscal transactions with the federal government. This calculation was made taking into account Quebec's net fiscal balance (the difference between federal spending in Quebec and federal taxes paid in Quebec) as well as by making adjustments and corrections required by fiscal tax credits, the federal budget deficit and debt service.

According to Statistics Canada, in 1992 Ottawa spent $956 more per capita in Quebec than it collected in taxes in Quebec. By comparison, Ottawa spent $215 more per capita in Ontario and $5,833 more per capita in Prince Edward Island than it collected in those two provinces; Alberta and British Columbia paid more in taxes than they received from Ottawa! Since

1970, Quebec has always received more than it paid and Alberta has always received less than it paid.

Statistics naturally vary from study to study, as we will see shortly. But no single serious study can demonstrate that Quebec loses out, in terms of federal spending.

Although we know some readers may find statistics hard to digest, we submit the following information so that readers may draw their own conclusions.

Once the necessary adjustments are made, as the first Infometrica has done (*La Presse,* November 15, 1994), we arrive at the conclusion that each Ontarian contributed $1400 more to the federal budget than he or she received, while Quebec made a slight gain of $250 per capita and Prince Edward Island a gain of $5,629 per capita.

Moreover, according to a 1994 study by the Fraser Institute, we see that Quebec made a net gain in terms of federal spending, since it received $696 more per capita on average from the federal government than it paid out in taxes (Walker, 1994).

In other words, if we rely on these calculations, which back up the position taken by André Raynauld, we can conclude that Quebec received more than it paid out in 1993. Depending on the calculation method used, this net gain for Quebeckers runs from $2.34 billion to $5.07 billion. The very conservative figure of $2.34 billion was derived using the number of Quebec taxpayers (3.33 million). But we can conclude that Quebec gained $5.07 billion, by using the net gain per capita figure of $696, used by Mr. Walker of the Fraser Institute (Walker, 1994).

Quebec receives more than its "fair share" in transfers, but the fair-share argument is not necessarily appropriate, since it cuts both ways

The Bloc Québécois has often claimed, particularly during the 1993 election campaign, that Quebec received less than Ontario. For example, Lucien Bouchard maintained that Quebec did not get its fair share of federal spending in the sectors of agriculture, regional development and research and development.

An analysis of transfers for the year 1993-94 reveals however that Quebec received more from the federal government than its share of the Canadian population (25 %) (Table 11) or than its share in the Canadian economy (22.5 % of GDP) (Table 2).

But according to Aurèle Beaulnes, scientist and president of the firm GMCNI Inc., it is time to challenge the principle so often used by indépendantistes that Quebec must get its "fair share" from the federal government. The "fair-share" principle is a dangerous and irrational principle that cuts both ways. Excellence - not demographics - should be the sole competitive criterion on which to base decisions on the allocation of limited funds. Let us take culture and science for example. What is one to make of the fact that in country-wide competition, Quebec's artistic community gets 30 % of available funds and Quebec's scientific community 37 %? Should funding for these two Quebec communities be held at 25 %? But that would mean an annual loss of $100 million for the science sector and $45 million for culture.

We have often heard however that Quebec does not receive its "fair share" of 25 % of federal funding in science and technology. In Ottawa, Bloc Québécois MP Gilles Duceppe quoted the figure of 11 %, while other MPs quoted the figure of 18 %. But Aurèle Beaulnes points out that *"a rigorous and global analysis of all contracts, contributions and subsidies in the sector of research and development and related scientific activities shows that Quebec's private sector obtains about 30 %. This amount is higher than the usual parametres used to determine the 'fair share': 25 % of Canada's population, 23 % of its GDP, and 22 % of its scientific labor force."* (For a complete description of Quebec's share in research and development, see Aurèle Beaulnes, 1994).

In terms of regional development, the most complete study was conducted by Gérald Bernier in *Bilan québécois du fédéralisme canadien* (Bernier: 1992). This study ranges from 1970 to 1989, and indicates that Quebec received its fair share and more, over the last few years.

But figures can be manipulated. They can be made to say whatever one wants, as is shown by the examples of agriculture as well as of research and development.

Throughout the 1993 federal election campaign, Mr. Bouchard claimed that Quebec did not get its fair share of federal spending on either agriculture or research and development. Political scientist Stéphane Dion has studied spending on agriculture between 1985 and 1992. His study shows that the share of federal spending to support the agrofood business, measured as a percentage of the agrofood GDP, was 19 % across Canada and 8 % in Quebec. Ontario for its part only got 7 %. The lion's share going to grain producers in the West because of the dramatic drop in their earnings (Dion, 1993: B-3).

Moreover, the federal government also plays an active role in coordinating the national system of demand management, which is particularly advantageous for milk producers, many of whom are concentrated in Quebec. These Quebec milk producers also receive subsidies from Canadian consumers, thanks to federal regulations.

As for support of research and development, figures from Statistics Canada show that Quebec and Ontario respectively receive about 29 % and 50 % of total federal spending. But the funds headed for Ontario are largely allocated to laboratories and agencies of the federal government, many of which are located in Ottawa. This is a case of internal accounting, by which the federal government finances its own agencies, which serve all Canadians. If these funds destined for federal agencies are substracted from the total amount, Quebec's share of spending is just as high as that of other provinces.

Figures produced by the Bloc Québécois in 1993 on investments by ministries and federal government purchases should also be corrected. When the indépendantistes complain of a "systematic bias" in favor of Ontario, they are ignoring the fact that such programs require some concentration in order to work properly. "If this type of accounting were applied to Quebec," concludes Stéphane Dion, "then all Quebec regions would be justified in revolting against the so-called special treatment granted to Quebec City." (Dion, 1993: B-3).

Quebec receives more than Ontario

"The theory according to which the federal government serves first and foremost the interests of Ontario is mistaken when it comes to tax flows and expenses." (Raynauld, 1990:7).

Indeed, with 25 % of the Canadian population and 22.5 % of its GDP, Quebec gets much more than Ontario, which has 37 % of the population and 40 % of its GDP.

In 1993-1994, Quebec received $7.8 billion in cash transfers out of a total of $29 billion.

Furthermore, tax-point transfers corresponding to taxes collected in Quebec amounted in 1993-1994 to $3.72 billion (out of a total of $11.52 billion) (Table 4).

These transfers were mainly part of three programs: equalization payments, Established Programs Financing or EPF (health and post-secondary education) and the Canada Assistance Plan (social welfare and social services) (Ministry of Finance of Canada, 194 a:6, see Table 3).

These transfers are not simply welfare cheques. They contribute to job creation. That is particularly the case of financial assistance in the fields of health and post-secondary education, which account for half of all transfers to the provinces.

Quebec gets the lion's share of equalization payments, or 46.2 % of all equalization payments made in 1993-94 by the federal government ($3.8 billion out of $8.5 billion). Ontario gets nothing at all, since it has its own fiscal resources, as do Alberta and British Columbia (see Tables 4 and 5). Equalization is a Canadian invention which helps support the revenues of provincial governments and which they can use as they see fit.

When it comes to the EPF (health and post-secondary education), Quebec received $540 per capita, while Ontario only received $400 (see Table 6).

Finally, with respect to the Canada Assistance Plan, Quebec receives 34.6 % of all federal transfers in this plan, while

Ontario only gets 30.6 %. The breakdown per capita shows a far wider gap between the two provinces, however. Quebec receives $380 per capita (more than any other province) and Ontario receives $230 per capita (less than any other province). The difference is due to the effect of different programs (tax points, fiscal transfers, etc.) in the calculation of the Canada Assistance Plan (Ministry of Finance of Canada, 1994c:28).

TABLE 1
POPULATION OF QUEBEC AND ONTARIO

Population of Canada	29,248,100 (July 1, 1993)
Population of Quebec	7,281,000 (July 1, 1994)
Percentage/Canada	25 %
COMPARISON	
Population of Ontario	10,927,800 (July 1, 1994)
Percentage/Canada	37 %

TABLE 2: QUEBEC'S GDP

Quebec	$ 160 billion (1993)
Canada	$ 710 billion (1993)
Percentage/Canada	22,5 %
Ontario	$ 285 billion (1993)
Percentage/Canada	40 %

TABLE 3: FEDERAL CASH TRANSFERS TO QUEBEC

Cash tranfers are paid out as follows:

Equalization	$ 3.8 billion
Welfare	$ 2.0 billion
Fiscal Agreements	$ 1.7 billion
Other	$ 231 million
TOTAL	$ 7.8 billion

Source: (Quebec Ministry of Finance, 1994: 11).

TABLE 4
FEDERAL CASH TRANSFERS AND TAX POINTS
FOR QUEBEC AND ONTARIO

	COMPARAISON	
PROGRAMS	QUEBEC	ONTARIO
FPE	5,348	8,023
Equalization	3,724	0
CAP	2,800	2,528
TOTAL	11,522	10,551

Source: (Ministry of Finance of Canada, 1994d).

TABLE 5
FEDERAL TRANSFERS TO THE PROVINCES

PROGRAMS	
Epf	21,476
Equalization	8,500
CAP	8,050

These figures include cash transfers (established program funding, the Canada Assistance Plan and equalization) and tax points.

Other	4,700
TOTAL	41,910

Source: (Ministère des Finances du Canada, 1994d).

74

TABLE 6: EPF COMPARISON QUEBEC/ONTARIO
PER CAPITA (IN MILLIONS OF 1994 $)

	QUEBEC	ONTARIO
Tax points	$ 380	$ 400
Equalization	20	0
Tax rebates	140	0
TOTAL	540	400

Source: (Ministry of Finance of Canada, 1994d).

SECOND PART OF THE MYTH: FEDERALISM COSTS A LOT BECAUSE OF OVERLAPS AND DUPLICATION

What they tell us: *"Federalism costs a lot because of overlaps and duplication. Independence would result in savings."*

Reality: the savings that independence would bring about are greatly exaggerated

A serious examination of the question of overlaps and duplication can only lead to the following conclusion: while overlaps and duplication exist in Canada, the savings that independence would bring about are greatly exaggerated, as we will see.

Moreover, it is interesting to note that when people talk of savings obtained as a result of separation, they forget two facts: federalism offers the advantage of economies of scale, and most overlaps are not at the federal-provincial level but at the provincial-provincial level, since that is where the growth of public administration has largely taken place.

The costs of duplication and federal-provincial overlaps are greatly exaggerated.

The general public wants governments to save money by cutting the costs of operations, and demands that public spending be rationalized. As for the indépendantistes, they point the finger at federal-provincial duplication, as if it were the main source of waste. Let us analyze this claim.

We will take as our source of information the most detailed study ever undertaken on the subject: "Overlaps and duplication of federal and provincial programs" (Treasury Board, 1991). In 1991, the Canadian government did a careful study of overlaps by rigorously examining all Canadian government programs. The Treasury Board did its study on the basis of federal government spending items contained in the budget of the Government of Canada for the fiscal year 1991-92. In addition, the Board examined the activities of comparable administrations in the provinces and territories. The managers of federal programs assessed to what extent federal programs offered the same services or responded to the needs of the same clients. Besides, the Board asked one hundred organizations (particularly national and regional business and industry associatons, universities and independent research establishments) to submit their views on overlaps and duplication. Senior civil servants working for key provincial agencies also took part in the study.

Before we launch into the Treasury Board study, we should note that there is often confusion between duplication and overlaps, which are actually two different things:

- We can speak of duplication when two levels of government intervene in the same sector to offer services to the same clients, and when the withdrawal of one level of government would have no effect on the person receiving those services.

- We can speak of an overlap when two levels of government intervene in the same sector to offer services to similar clients.

HERE ARE SOME OF THE MOST IMPORTANT CONCLUSIONS:

(1) There is much less duplication of programs than people believe

Listening to the way some people talk, one would almost think that thousands of federal civil servants do exactly the same thing as Quebec civil servants. The reality is that there is relatively little duplication: federal and provincial programs offering the same services to the same clients amount to a small fraction of the total expenses of the federal administration (no more than 1.3 %). To understand how much that represents, it should be noted that a 1 % rise in interest rates places a much heavier burden on federal spending (because of debt service) than duplication does. While it is important to reduce duplication, the total elimination of duplication would have only a marginal effect on government finances.

(2) Besides, when there are overlaps, that is because the levels of government offer complementary rather than competing services.

A certain amount of overlaps can be found in every federal state, especially considering that some problems, such as AIDS, the environment and trade, call for both national and provincial responses. The former chief justice of the Supreme Court, Brian Dickson, wrote:

> *"In a federal system, it is inevitable that, in pursuing valid objectives, the legislation of each level of government will impact occasionally on the sphere of power of the other."*

Overlaps of federal and provincial programs amount to 42 % of federal programs. Although no precise figures were available, the authors of the study concluded that to a large extent the two levels of government act in the same sector in a complementary fashion, which enables them to attain compatible objectives or to reinforce the role played by the other government. In many areas, the presence of two governments in the same sector of activity has doubtless meant the public has obtained better services than if just one government acted alone. In the case of federal-provincial cost-shared programs in the health sector, for example, federal transfers enable the provinces to offer the same quality of services (Treasury Board, 1991:8, 21, 23).

In addition, in sectors where the risk of useless overlaps is high, governments have sought to respect the limitations and objectives of other administrations and to target their respective actions. As a result, each level of government completes the action of the other level of government. Let us take the example of parks: at first sight, one may have the impression that federal and provincial programs overlap each other. The network of federal parks aims to conserve the best sample of each of Canada's 39 natural regions, and is designed for public access and nature interpretation. But provincial parks are designed for leisure and much less for conservation and nature interpretation (Treasury Board, 1991:22).

Another example is agriculture. In this sector, in Quebec, the federal and provincial governments both have a veterinary hygiene program. But the programs have different objectives. The federal program is designed to meet international and commercial objectives. It includes inspections and quarantines at border posts, in order to control the health of animals headed for export and import and to prevent the introduction of certain contagious diseases. The Quebec program meanwhile is essentially designed to provide economic support at the local level: this program transfers funds to veterinarians for the provision of services to the province's livestock.

Savings to be achieved by merging the two levels of government: a poor reason to declare independence

It could be argued and with reason that in some cases it would be easier to transfer the administration of particular programs to a single level of government. In the 1950s, for example, Quebec decided to have its own tax-collection system, while in the rest of Canada, the federal government collects not only federal taxes, but also provincial taxes which it redistributes to the provinces.

Nobody denies that it would be worthwhile to remove some of these administrative overlaps, since a straight transfer would bring about some savings. But we would find it easier to agree with the no-overlaps view if it didn't imply that every transfer of power has to be from the federal government to the provincial government, the way indépendantistes claim, when they demand that all powers be invested in the Quebec government.

And when a straight transfer proves impossible, why not show a little innovative spirit? A national tax commission could be set up as a non-governmental body, with the goal of managing tax-collection at the federal and provincial levels.

Some people believe that independence would result in substantial savings. But it is important to analyze the entire question of savings and to ensure that the proposed changes would actually make things work in a more efficient fashion. Unfortunately, by taking for granted that all transfers must automatically favor the provincial government, people forget to ask what would be the best level of government to administer a given program.

In addition, the argument that independence would bring about savings by merging two levels of government is a weak one. As we will see, independence would not bring about savings, but would actually create duplication in new areas.

1) Since the Second World War, provincial governments have grown considerably and have set up interprovincial coordinating mechanisms, in order to lessen provincial-provincial duplication. Independence would actually increase duplication.

Since the Second World War, Canadians have witnessed growth in provincial and municipal administration. In 1950, for example, the federal government spent $1.93 for each dollar spent by the provinces. This figure dropped to $1.08 in 1970 and $1.07 in 1990. In 1950, the federal government earmarked $2.36 for the purchase of goods and services (without counting transfers and debt service) for every dollar spent by the provinces. In 1970, this figure had tumbled to $1.09 and in 1990 to $0.72 (Treasury Board, 1991:40).

The larger these provincial administrations became, the more provinces sought to coordinate their efforts, to diminish the relatively little-known problem of provincial-provincial duplication. This coordination was important since each province was doing exactly the same thing. Let us take the example of the environment, since pollution does not respect provincial borders. Or the example of health, since all provinces face the same challenge, namely how to ensure "free" medical services to the general public and how even to improve the quality of those services, with less and less money.

Although the provinces have made an inadequate effort to join their forces, that effort is nonetheless indispensable. If indépendantistes were serious about the desire to rationalize government operations, they would strive to pool certain provincial services, to make them more efficient and less costly. Instead of that, indépendantistes intend to create a new level of government, aggravating existing duplication and making it impossible to coordinate provincial-provincial activites.

2) The Canadian public sector is not larger than that of some unitary states, such as France and Great Britain. Quebec independence would lead to a bloated bureaucracy.

We are told that having a single level of government would diminish the size of the public sector and make the State more efficient. That position is debatable.

Canada, a federal country with two levels of government, has a public sector proportionately smaller than in most industrial countries organized as unitary states. As a result, in Canada, the different levels of government employ a little less than 19 % of the total active population, or less than OECD countries such as France (25.4 %) and Great Britain (19.9 %, Treasury Board, 1991:38).

Once Quebec became independent, it would have to increase the size of the Quebec bureaucracy, in order to deliver services that the federal goovernment delivered previously.

3) Belonging to a federation results in economies of scale. By separating, Quebec will have to duplicate services it currently provides together with the federal government, and will thereby lose the economies of scale offered by the current federal system.

There is no point in seeking to justify Quebec independence on the grounds that it will result in savings, by avoiding duplication. In fact, Quebec will have to deliver the same services as the provincial and federal governments currently do, while simultaneously starting from scratch to build an entire new governmental structure.

The merger of two levels of government would result in additional costs, not only because Quebec's bureaucracy would grow larger, but also because Quebec would lose the advantage of economies of scale.

By separating, Quebec would have to deliver services currently offered by the federal government, and could no longer profit from economies of scale resulting from the sharing of fixed costs and the rationalization made possible by having services in common with the nine other provinces.

There are many examples of such savings: one Ministry of Foreign Affairs instead of ten, one Ministry of Defence, embassies, consulates, border controls, an army. Belonging to the federation means these services can be offered together and on a large scale. Many benefits cannot be quantified, such as shared public resources, foreign currency, infrastructures and above all economies of scale. By increasing volumes, economies of scale bring down unit costs. A good example is the Canadian transportation system, which includes railways, highways and transport by air and sea. In the sector of energy and particularly of natural gas, Quebec pays less than its share of costs and thus obtains a continual and permanent form of equalization subsidy. In the telecommunications sector, the same analysis applies. Economies of scale reduce the operating costs for Quebec and open up its access to the Information Superhighway, providing many advantages.

As a result, by duplicating federal services, individual Quebeckers will see their fixed costs rise. All the savings that Quebec is supposed to derive from having a single level of government will be more than made up for by the loss of savings resulting from "repatriating" federal powers as well as by the subsequent expansion of the Quebec bureaucracy. Moreover, the creation of new ministries and hiring all federal civil servants from Quebec in the "new Quebec civil service" (as the Parti Québécois promises to do) will lead to a rise in the cost of services.

CONCLUSION

Those people who think that independence is necessary to save money have latched on to a mistaken position. As we have seen above, Quebec has profited handsomely from its membership in the Canadian federation. Quebec has received more than its 25 % share of the country's population might call for, and more than other provinces (like Ontario). It is moreover a mistake to claim that independence would eliminate overlaps and duplication. In fact, the savings that can be achieved are highly exaggerated and merging the two levels of government, far from bringing about substantial savings, would probably lead to higher costs for Quebeckers.

Even though we have just shown that this myth lacks any basis in fact, we are nonetheless convinced that a straight "accounting" approach to Quebec's place in Canada is a tortuous labyrinth. Since the figures are complex and many variables enter into play, people can end up with different results.

So, in order to simplify the debate, we will conclude by saying that Quebec benefits handsomely from being a part of Canada - but that the advantages it enjoys go well beyond any straight addition of columns of figures. The numerous advantages that Quebec enjoys are sometimes more subtle than that, and make it all the more important to maintain federal links with Canada.

It is therefore absurd to advocate separation in order to save money and to eliminate duplication and overlaps. If this argument is carried to its logical conclusion, then the ten provinces should all separate in order to reduce their operating costs. And then each region within each province should do the same. We would end up with something like medieval manors from feudal times, both self-sufficient and ... poor.

A serious analysis leads us to conclude that every organization including nation-states has an optimal size. If the challenge is to govern the more than one billion Chinese, then perhaps the country should be divided up into smaller units. But Canada, with its 29 million inhabitants, has exactly the opposite problem, and that is why pooling our efforts is needed to achieve economies of scale. An independent Quebec with 7 million inhabitants would suffer from not being able to achieve significant economies of scale and would be too small to be effective.

Myth 4: AN INDEPENDENT QUEBEC WILL EASILY GET OUT OF PAYING CANADA'S DEBT

Context

In 1991, a study submitted to the Bélanger-Campeau Commission suggested that in the event Quebec separated, the Quebec share of the federal debt should be between 17 and 19 %, as we will see shortly (Bélanger-Campeau, 1991: 476-482). This proved to be a highly controversial suggestion, since Quebec's share in Canada's gross domestic product is 22.5 % and its share in Canada's population is 25 %. In Spring 1994, Jacques Parizeau even went so far as to claim that an independent Quebec would be under no obligation to pay the interest on this debt. These carefree claims, this juggling with billions of dollars, give the general public the impression that Canada's debt is not Quebec's problem, and that an independent Quebec could back out of its financial obligations if it chose to.

In actual fact, the question of dividing up the debt is a very important and always painful one. If things go well, debt can be calmly divided. If things go badly, it can lead to serious disputes, not to mention grave conflicts. In the dramatic context of Quebec separation, where all of Canada would have to absorb the devastating and brutal aftershocks produced by the geographic, social, commercial and financial shattering of the country, it hardly seems probable that the negotiating atmosphere would be relaxed. The bitter discussions over dividing up the debt in the former Czechoslovakia (which is considered to have pulled off a "velvet" divorce) and the uncertainty and economic havoc witnessed during this period, lead us to believe that Quebec and the rest of Canada would be severely jolted in ways we cannot now foresee.

There are two important studies on the state of public finances in an independent Quebec and on the resulting division of federal debt. Both date back to 1991: the first was conducted by the secretariat of the Bélanger-Campeau Commission, the second by the Economic Council of Canada. In September 1994, the Fraser Institute also conducted a study on the division of the debt, although some of the methodology it used proved very controversial. Nevertheless, we will use the perfectly reasonable parts of the study (Richardson, 1994).

But before starting, it is indispensable that we lay out what is at stake in the division of the debt. It is by understanding the macro-economic stakes that the debate surrounding the different methods proposed can best be understood. We will therefore start by discussing the economic stakes of the division of the debt, and their possible impact on the public finances both of Quebec and of the rest of Canada. Then we will analyze the conclusions of the secretariat of the Bélanger-Campeau Commission and the critical reaction to those conclusions. In our own conclusion, we will try to offer a synthesis of the two divergent points of view.

THE ECONOMIC STAKES IN THE DIVISION OF THE DEBT

The division of the national debt is by nature a contentious issue, since whatever one party wins, the other party will lose

Whatever formula is adopted to divide up the debt, an independent Quebec would find itself with both a higher debt and absolute deficit than it had previously. An important question is whether, in the event of independence, the indebtedness per capita of Quebeckers and other Canadians would be higher than it is now. In fact, whatever one party gained in terms of advantageous conditions, the other party would lose by having a heavier debt load (Economic Council of Canada, 1991:87). As we will see later on, it is probable that Quebec would not be in a position of force in its negotiations on the division of the debt, which means it is foreseeable that the division would not be to Quebec's advantage.

It is for this reason that the division of the national debt is a contentious issue. If, following the division, the level of indebtedness *per capita* of one of the parties rises, then the interest payments on its public debt will represent a higher percentage of its public expenses. The people will then have to support a higher deficit and debt load.

The party that loses out in negotiations will have to resort to taxes and loans to finance its debt

Governments traditionally resort to four sources of revenue to finance their debt: taxes, loans taken out through the sale of government bonds, the sale of public assets and the creation of new money by increasing the monetary base. In the event that Quebec separated, the injured party would favor the first two sources of revenue, and would be under the obligation to raise taxes and sell more government bonds. There are fewer public assets to sell off since the wave of privatizations that started in Canada in the mid-1980s. Creating new money as a means of financing deficits would be an inflationary policy, and one frowned upon by the financial markets. Tax increases both for individuals and companies, in order to finance interest payments on the public debt, would lead to a drop in consumer spending and would increase the production costs of companies, which would become less competitive and much less likely to make investments. All of which would slow economic growth.

The sale of government securites to finance new deficits would raise interest rates and slow the economic growth of national production. The government would have a higher level of indebtedness after independence, and would be required to raise interest rates to finance its deficit, in order to attract capital coming both from domestic and foreign investors.

Increasing the level of indebtedness and creating a new political entity would increase the risk premium and would bring about a massive rise in interest rates

The risk premium has three components: the political risk, the risk associated with exchange rates and the risk of default. It is important to underline the fact that risk premiums, and particularly the political risk, would probably be higher for Quebec, whatever the level of indebtedness of the Quebec government after sovereignty. An independent Quebec would be a new political entity and would have a smaller economy than the rest of Canada, and would therefore be more vulnerable to economic disruption.

1) The risk of default

Grouping together interprovincial risks of default in a federation reduces the individual risk of default of each of the provinces. Indeed, the federal government has a larger fiscal base and thus a more reliable source of revenue than the provinces taken separately. This explains why bonds issued by the federal government are rated triple A, since its solvency is greater than that of the provinces, which means it can borrow at lower interest rates than the provinces. By transferring part of their risks to the federal government, the provinces reduce their debt-service payments. This economy of scale was one of the principle reasons the four original provinces joined together in 1867. Any division of the federal debt between Quebec and the rest of Canada would make the total service of the debt more difficult and would increase the risk of default of both parties, which would have to rely on a smaller tax base and therefore on a less reliable source of revenue than is currently the case with the federal government (Economic Council of Canada, 1991:88).

Any structural change would cause financial markets to re-evaluate the solvency of the new governments, using four criteria: the debt/GDP ratio, the tax burden, the economic outlook and the existence of loan guarantees at a higher level of government (Economic Council of Canada 1991:86-88).

The first three criteria are interrelated. If one of the parties had a higher debt/GDP ratio than it currently does, then it would be forced to increase the tax burden and its economic outlook would be less promising as a result. In short, an unfavorable division of the debt would increase the risk of default of one of the parties. As far as the fourth criterion is concerned, Quebec alone would be affected, since the federal government would no longer provide guarantees for Quebec's debt, which would reduce the solvency of the Quebec government and increase the costs of borrowing.

2) The political risk

The political risk is linked to uncertainty over the potential impact of political changes on fiscal policy, on the return of investments and capital flows and on macro-economic policies. In 1976, for example, when the Parti Québécois was elected, there was a 60-base-point difference in Canada between Quebec and Ontario bonds, and a 100-base-point difference in the United States. This difference reached a high point during the first nine months after the election, but gradually came down to 0 after two years (Economic Council of Canada, 1991:86).

3) The risk associated with exchange rates

Financial markets would also evaluate possible fluctuations in the value of the Canadian dollar brought on by the new monetary policies of the new governments. They would assess the possibility of a collapse of the monetary union between Quebec and the rest of Canada. As a result, investors would demand higher interest rates on Canadian and Quebec bonds to compensate for the increased risk associated with assets in Canadian dollars.

The separation of Quebec would bear a substantial economic cost, since a small entity would be more vulnerable to economic disruption

The rest of Canada and above all Quebec itself would have to raise interest rates. The two parties would have, first, to adopt more restrictive monetary policies than those currently in place, and, second, to offer higher interest rates. Besides, the government whose debt level increased after the division of the debt would have to offer interest rates higher than the risk premiums demanded by investors.

The rise in interest rates on government bonds would bring about an increase in real interest rates as well as a drop in both private investment expenses and national production. In addition, purchases of government bonds by foreign investors would increase demand for the Canadian dollar (or new Quebec dollar), which would result in lower net exports and national production. According to estimates made by the Economic Council of Canada, an increase of 100 base points in real interest rates would bring about a permanent loss of some 1.5 % of Canada's long-term gross domestic product (Economic Council of Canada, 1991:85-86).

In the event of separation, Quebec and the rest of Canada would have to bear very heavy economic costs associated with risk premiums, which would be highest of all for Quebec. The economic costs associated with sovereignty would multiply, if, after the debt was divided, there was an increase in the level of indebtedness of one of the parties. The party that seemed to have the upper hand in the division of the debt would not necessarily win out in the end. By impoverishing its primary exchange partner, the "winning" party could see its exports and national production suffer as a result.

We will now examine the different formulas for the division of the federal debt, proposed both by the secretariat of the Bélanger-Campeau Commission and by its critics.

THE DIFFERENT DEBT-DIVISION FORMULAS

The formula proposed by the secretariat of the Bélanger-Campeau Commission: an independent Quebec would be in a position to assume its share of the debt, the way small European countries do

The secretariat of the Bélanger-Campeau Commission proposed in 1991 that the government of an independent Quebec should assume a share of liabilities directly proportional to the share of assets it inherited. In terms of public spending, assets generate revenues while liabilities involve costs. According to those international experts consulted, the accounting methods used by the secretariat to divide the assets and liabilities of the federal government would be in line with the current state of international law.

In preparing three scenarios for the division of assets and liabilities, the secretariat made an estimate of the state of public finances of the Government of Quebec, based on revenues and expenses in the fiscal year 1990-91. The secretariat drew up a main scenario (A) as well as two backup scenarios (B) and (C), which are variations on the main scenario. These latter two scenarios take into account uncertainty about the real value of non-financial assets held by the federal public administration, as well as about Quebec's share of these assets.

On March 31, 1990, federal liabilities amounted to $399 billion while financial assets amounted to $41 billion. However, there had been no recent estimate of the market value of non-financial or non-physical assets (Economic Council of Canada, 1991:87).

The secretariat noted that the main scenario pegged Quebec's share of the federal debt at 18.5 %. But it said the method of calculation used to assess non-financial assets could make a difference of plus or minus 1.5 %. As a result, according to the backup scenarios (B) and (C), Quebec's share is pegged at 19.5 % and 17 % respectively (Bélanger-Campeau, 1991: 476-482). These variations would affect budgetary expenses, particularly those related to debt service and to the budget deficit.

We will now look at the figures provided in scenario A for the deficit and debt service. The deficit of the Government of Quebec would increase from 1.2 % to 5.8 % of GDP; meanwhile, the deficit of the rest of Canada would slip from 4.5 % to 4.4 % of its GDP (see Table 2). Expressed as a percentage of GDP, the Government of Quebec's debt service would increase from 2.8 % to 7.2 %, while the same percentage for the rest of Canada would increase from 6.3 % to 6.8 % (see Table 2).

Quebec's debt would amount to 56 % of its GDP (see Graph 1). If this percentage is compared to percentages for European countries such as Austria and Denmark or indeed for most Western countries, Quebec's debt/GDP ratio does not seem excessive. As for the rest of Canada, it would end up with a debt equivalent to 65.6 % of its GDP. The secretariat concluded on the basis of its formula for the division of the debt, that an independent Quebec would be in a position to assume its share of the debt, the way small European countries do.

We will now examine the criticism levelled at the secretariat's conclusions.

Formulas developed by critics: Quebec would not be in the same situation as small European countries and would have a hard time taking on an increased level of indebtedness

Critics of the Bélanger-Campeau Commission's conclusions rightly challenged the methods used by the secretariat as well as its conclusions. According to the critics, Quebec would be in a different situation than small European countries and would have a hard time taking on an increased level of indebtedness.

1) The rules on division set by the Bélanger-Campeau Commission are debatable

In the event that Quebec separated, it would be necessary to assess the assets and liabilities of the federal government. But there are no clear rules in international law governing the way to divide up debt in such a situation. According to Thomas Courchene, the rest of Canada would never accept the method proposed by the secretariat, since it does not take into account interprovincial revenue transfers by means of equalization payments, which over the last few decades have largely benefitted Quebec. Mr. Courchene adds that the secretariat's formula is mistaken, since deficits contribute directly to liabilities and not to assets. Indeed, leaving aside physical assets, deficits have been used to finance manpower training and consumption, neither of which shows up in the secretariat's calculations (Courchene, 1991:25-29).

2) Three other possible criteria for dividing up the debt

The Economic Council proposes three criteria for dividing up the debt:

- A demographic criterion: since the population of Quebec accounts for about 25 % of Canada's total population, the debt could be divided up on a 1/4 - 3/4 basis. Each Canadian would have an equal burden.

- The criterion of solvency: the capacity of each province to pay, based on the GDP and on federal revenue collected.

- An accountability criterion: the share corresponding to the proportion of the debt contracted by the federal government on behalf of each province over the years.

In Table 1, we can see the results of dividing up the debt using these three criteria: Quebec's share would be between 21 % and 31 %, the average being 23.9 %. According to the Economic Council, Quebec would have to take on a share of the debt close to its share of Canada's population and GDP, namely between 23 % and 25 %. This division would bring Quebec's debt/GDP ratio well above the 56.5 % figure foreseen by the secretariat. Unfortunately, the Economic Council does not provide a precise percentage (Economic Council of Canada, 1991:86).

People opposed to the Bélanger-Campeau formula admit that an independent Quebec would be economically viable, but that the transition would be long and painful. According to them, Quebec cannot be compared to small European countries in demo-economic terms. The Netherlands and Switzerland, for example, became independent nations before the welfare state was created, when their respective populations were growing and contributing to their economic prosperity. Some people consider that the probable departure of some Quebeckers after independence would result in a smaller Quebec population. The Government of Quebec's tax base would be smaller as a result. It would then be difficult to maintain current social programs, at a time when Quebec would be facing a proportionately higher level of indebtedness.

Would an independent Quebec be able to finance its share of the federal debt?

Quebec's share of the federal debt would be around $110 billion, and it would have to finance an annual deficit in the neighborhood of $15 billion (one quarter of the federal government's current debt and deficit). The Quebec government would have a hard time financing this debt load for three reasons: Quebec's current level of indebtedness is already high; independence would reduce the tax base that the government would partly use to finance its debt; and in technical terms it would be very difficult to expand the market of Quebec government bonds. We will examine each of these variables.

It would be very difficult for an independent Quebec to carry an additional debt load, since its current net level of indebtedness (127.1 % of GDP) is very high compared to that of the rest of Canada. Indeed, the net indebtedness of an independent Quebec would rise to 149.4 % of GDP (Richardson, 1994: 33).

An independent Quebec would have to expand the market of Quebec government bonds in order to finance its share of the federal debt, since it would be cut off from Ottawa's financial machine. At the present time, the federal government is able to finance its debt and an annual deficit of $40 billion, by using the financial markets it has developed for this purpose over the last few decades. In order to expand the market of Quebec bonds, the government would likely have to offer preferential interest rates in order to attract investors. As a result, interest rates would rise, bringing about a drop in investments and increased unemployment.

CONCLUSION

It is probable that an independent Quebec would be economically viable on the mid and long term, but it would no longer be as prosperous. The division of the debt would worsen the state of public finances in Quebec and the rest of Canada and would result in significant economic costs for both parties, which would have a weaker reputation for solvency, higher interest rates, a drop in investment expenses, a heavier tax burden, reduced net exports, etc. These costs would probably be higher for Quebec than for the rest of the country, given Quebec's already high tax burden and its smaller and less diversified economy, as well as its greater vulnerability to economic disruption, due to shocks in the business cycle or to external factors. The losses associated with independence would increase in proportion to the rise in the level of indebtedness of one of the parties.

Quebec would have to take on a share of the federal debt in the neighborhood of 25 % for two reasons. First, Quebec is more dependent in trade terms on the rest Canada than the other way round. And second, the rest of Canada would probably never accept the method of dividing the debt proposed by the Bélanger-Campeau Commission, according to which Quebec's share of the debt would amount to some 18.5 %.

In an ideal world, an independent Quebec could dream of gradually and calmly taking on its share of the federal debt over a well-defined period, so that it was better able to finance its own higher deficits. The Government of Quebec would want to take the time it needed to develop expanded financial markets for its bonds and thus to reduce premiums as well as Quebec's risk of default.

But the division of debt brings with it the risk of creating thorny and difficult problems. There could be no "velvet" and painless divorce. It should be remembered that in the game of debt division, whatever some parties win, others will lose. If Quebec takes on a small proportion of the federal debt, then the rest of Canada will have to take on a larger one; it is simply an illusion, therefore, to count on abundant good faith and generosity at the bargaining table. Negotiations would be both difficult and extremely bitter.

The division of debt is complicated by the very high level of Canadian debt, the greater part of which is held outside of the country. Those people who imagine that dividing the debt is some simple accounting operation and that an independent Quebec could easily and painlessly get out of paying Canada's debt are taking their dreams for reality.

TABLE 1
SUPPLEMENTARY SCENARIOS - IMPACT OF THE VARIATION OF THE
VALUE OF NON-FINANCIAL ASSETS ON THE DIVISION OF THE BALANCE
SHEETS OF THE SUCCESSOR STATES

SCENARIO B

Succession balance sheets in 1989-1990		In %	Amount (millions of $)	Impact on budgetary spending 1990-91	
Financial assets	57 195	3.8*	2 169	Debt service:	
Non-financial assets	one dollar	—	—	Maturing debt	6 347
Total assets	57 195	3.8*	2 169	Other liabilities	152
Accumulated deficit	273 394	22.8	62 106		
TOTAL	329 589	19.5*	64 275		6 499

SCENARIO C

Financial assets	57 195	3.8*	2 169	Debt service:	
Non-financial assets	108 000	15.0-	16 200	Maturing debt	5 533
Total assets	165 195	11.1*	18 369	Other liabilities	132
Accumulated deficit	164 394	22.8	37 482		
TOTAL	329 589	17.0*	55 851		5 665

*Percentages derived from amounts.

TABLE 2
FINANCIAL INDICATORS*
ACCORDING TO BASE SCENARIO A

	QUEBEC		CANADA		FEDERAL GOVERNMENT	
	CURRENT	SCENARIO A	CURRENT	SCENARIO A	CURRENT	SCENARIO A
Deficit (1)						
Millions of $	-1 980	9 282	-37 323	-28 041	-30 500	-23 198
% GDP	1.3	5.8	5.5	5.4	4.5	4.4
Debt (2)						
% GDP	26.4	63.9	70.2	72.1	53.5	58.4
Debt service (3)						
% GDP	2.8	7.2	8.2	8.4	6.3	6.8
% of budgetary revenues	13.2	22.5	22.7	23.6	35.6	37.2

Scenario A: the federal governement and the nine provinces.

(1) In 1990-1991.

(2) Debt as of March 31, 1990: maturing debt and retirement pension accounts.

(3) Present-day Canada: the federal governement and the nine provinces.

Note: There is little point comparing Quebec's financial indicators as they would be in the succession of states scenarios, with those of the federal government, either at the present time, or in a scenario. Relevant comparisons can only be made between two entities having similar powers.

GRAPH 1:
QUEBEC-CANADA COMPARISON
GDP/DEBT* RATIO(%)

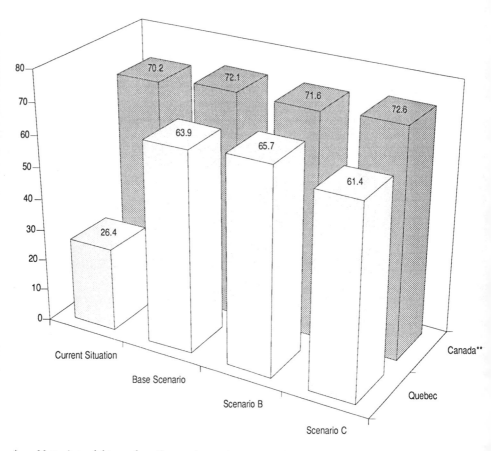

*   *Maturing debt and retirement pension accounts*
** *Present -day Canada: federal government and ten provinces; Canada scenario: federal government and nine provinces.*

Myth 5: AFTER INDEPENDENCE, THE QUEBEC-CANADA ECONOMIC UNION IS IN THE BAG

Context

The Parti Québécois has always come out in favor of the Canadian economic union, even though the governments of Quebec and other provinces sometimes throw up trade barriers that weaken the economic union. What would happen in the event that Quebec became independent? Is Quebec's membership in the Canadian economic union really "in the bag" the way indépendantistes claim? In order to answer this question, we will have to ask what type of relationship the PQ government would want to maintain with the rest of Canada after independence.

There is a lot of confusion over the ultimate objectives of the indépendantiste position, whether that confusion be intentional or not. In actual fact, a free-trade zone, a common market and an economic union are not one and the same thing. The degree of integration is different in each case, as are the means to attain the goal of integration.

A free-trade zone is a territory in which several countries or provinces eliminate all trade barriers between each other, while remaining free to impose customs tariffs. There are thus two kinds of barriers to free trade. The first comprises direct and visible rules, such as customs tariffs and import quotas. The second comprises non-tariff barriers, which are more subtle and much less apparent. A non-tariff trade barrier can be defined as: any law or practice that systematically favors local companies (government procurement policies, tax rebates, research and development subsidies). An example of a non-tariff barrier to free trade is the rule preventing the sale of beer from another country or province until such time as the beer company sets up a brewery in the place it wants to sell its beer. Nowadays, non-tariff barriers are much more powerful instruments of protectionism than customs tariffs themselves.

A real free-trade zone can only exist once these hidden barriers are eliminated.

A common market, meanwhile, exists where not only products but also production factors (natural resources, labor, capital, technologies) freely cross international and interprovincial boundaries. There is no common market if travellers need a passport or visa, or if capital transfers are controlled. Just as in the case of free trade, there are many kinds of hidden barriers to the circulation of production factors: restrictive linguistic policies, environmental standards, regulations concerning some professions. Between 1986 and 1992, Western Europe undertook to eliminate more than 200 hidden barriers that hindered the movement of people and capital, before moving onto the next stage, the Maastricht Treaty. That treaty calls for a much tighter integration of European countries.

Free trade and the common market are so-called "passive" kinds of economic integration, since they do not require joint initiatives, and rely essentially on the elimination of existing barriers, whether visible or invisible. On the other hand, more "active" approaches lead to an economic integration consisting of a customs union, a monetary union and an economic union. In a customs union, a joint customs tariff with respect to third parties is added to free trade. In a monetary union, nations adopt a common currency, maintain their respective currencies in fixed parity, and back up fixed parity with completely harmonized monetary policies.

A complete economic union of countries requires harmonized customs and monetary policies, coordinated social and even tax policies, and, in most cases, political integration on the federal or at least confederal model. Indeed, the absence of such mechanisms for joint decision-making brings about an imbalance: if all important decisions were taken by a supranational body, the regions would lack effective representation and would be politically marginalized. Thus, if an independent Quebec were bound by decisions taken in Ottawa, without having a chance to participate in the decision-making process, then an independent Quebec would be in an intolerable state of dependence. To avoid such a situation, economic unions are generally accompanied by political-integration mechanisms.

If one examines the statements of Jacques Parizeau and Lucien Bouchard, it looks as if the indépendantistes want to keep something midway between a complete economic union and a common market. But as we have seen, there is little point in maintaining an economic union without a political union. Quebec independence would bring an end to the complete economic union, which, in the best-case scenario, would be replaced by either a free-trade zone or a customs union. However, as we have seen already, Quebec would lose much of its influence by separating from the political union. Indeed, whereas Quebec's influence is now real, in the event of independence it would risk becoming symbolic. Although it may strike some people as a paradox, the best way for Quebec to maintain its influence as well as the competitive position of its companies is to strengthen Canada's existing economic union.

That is why we will examine whether the existing economic union can be improved. Then we will ask whether, in the event Quebec separated, a painless "reassociation" could be brought about. Finally, we will examine the impact of independence on the choice of currency as well as the fiscal consequences.

CONSEQUENCES OF INDEPENDENCE FOR THE QUEBEC-CANADA ECONOMIC UNION

Can the Quebec-Canada economic union really be improved?

The economic union linking Quebec to Canada is far from perfect, but it is worth mentioning that the provinces regularly work on eliminating trade barriers. This work is crucial. There may not be any tariff barriers between provinces, but there are hundreds of provincial policies and regulations that have the effect of hindering interprovincial trade. In addition, linguistic and professional barriers hinder the free circulation of people, which is an essential condition for a common market. As a result, labor is less mobile in Canada than in the United States, since Canadian workers in some professions have a hard time moving to regions where work is more abundant.

Another step needed to improve the economic union is to harmonize fiscal, budgetary and economic policies: in the past, some provinces adopted budgets to stimulate economic recovery, while others adopted austerity measures. Such contradictory policies send confused signals to financial markets, and end up discouraging investment. A European banker recently noted that the incongruous nature of the macro-economic policies of various levels of government, and particularly of the federal, Ontario and Quebec governments, had a negative impact. *"Imagine a patient admitted to the hospital with severe abdominal pain. The doctors recommend diametrically-opposed treatments. That's the best way to kill the patient. In Europe, meanwhile, we are harmonizing fiscal policies as a precondition to setting up a monetary union. In Canada, you have a monetary union and an orgy of contradictory fiscal policies. This situation needlessly weakens your economy."*

Fortunately, the Canadian economic union can be strengthened, and an encouraging sign is to be found in the work of various governments to improve the union. The solution is hardly to weaken the economic union, by bringing about Quebec independence, thus creating further disorder and differences between macro-economic policies. On the contrary, strengthening the Canadian economic union, through a greater harmonization of Canada's 11 governments, would make the country more competitive within NAFTA and the GATT. The example of European countries is particularly striking in this regard. The Maastricht Treaty means that European countries are embarked on strengthening their economic union, while voluntarily reducing national sovereignty.

It should be noted moreover that Quebec has a lot to lose from the disintegration of the Canadian economic space; it is therefore vital for Quebec to maintain trade with the rest of the country. Currently, Quebec is one of the provinces most dependent on the Canadian market. In 1989, 54.2 % of Quebec's total exports were headed for other Canadian provinces, while Ontario's exports to other Canadian provinces amounted to 44.8 %. Quebec, Manitoba and Prince Edward Island are the only Canadian provinces for which the domestic Canadian market is larger than the international market, when it comes to economic exchanges (Statistics Canada, 1993:3,6).

The position of the Parti Québécois and the Bloc Québécois is, to say the least, paradoxical. Both parties favor maintaining the Canadian economic space and especially the Quebec-Ontario trading area. By separating, Quebec would bring an end to the Canadian political union, and would deprive itself of federal harmonization and stabilization mechanisms, which alone can make the economic space work properly. That, in turn, would weaken Quebec's influence within a future "reassociation."

As we have already indicated, economic and political unions usually go together. A political union requires a central or federal State, with its own powers, to make it easier for joint policies to be developed. In the case of the European Union, for example, the Maastricht Treaty provides for the creation of community institutions with two goals in mind. First, to coordinate and more easily stabilize the social and economic policies of member states; and second, to make economic, monetary and democratic integration more effective (for example, by creating a central European bank, strengthening the powers of the European Parliament and creating a European Senate, creating a system of regional transfers, and coordinating fiscal and monetary policies, etc.)

For economic integration to be effective, it is crucial that the constitutional powers of the federal government and intergovernmental cooperation both enable the federal government to set up national standards and across-the-board harmonization. In Canada, the mobility and effective use of production factors is improved by standardizing financial norms and unemployment insurance, and by means of federal-provincial agreements in the areas of taxation, health, social welfare and pensions...

By separating, Quebec could no longer belong to the Canadian economic union as it currently exists, since an independent Quebec would deprive itself of all the mechanisms which ensure the existence of the economic union. But could an independent Quebec renegotiate a European-style economic union, with new, supranational institutions? Would an independent Quebec really be an unavoidable partner for the rest of Canada, making such an economic "reassociation" inevitable, the way the Parti Québécois and Bloc Québécois claim? Could reassociation be painless?

"Reassociation" would not automatically be painless

When one stops to consider the commercial power of attraction exerted by the United States on the rest of Canada (ROC) and on Quebec, one wonders whether it would be in the objective interests of ROC to negotiate an economic "reassociation" with Quebec after independence. In addition, there is no certainty that ROC and Quebec would be able to reach a friendly agreement. A Quebec pro-independence vote would create a great deal of distrust and anger in ROC. Just like Quebeckers, other Canadians are very proud of their country and would not respond warmly to any action which threatened the survival of their country.

It is probable that the other provinces would accept the results of a democratic choice in Quebec. But that would not prevent them from seeing Quebec independence as a destructive action, taken by a province which has profited handsomely from the existing federation. And it is in such a climate of "divorce" that the future relations of Canada and Quebec would be negotiated. That atmosphere would not be conducive to the spirit of confidence needed to negotiate a "reassociation" along the lines of the existing economic and monetary union. Negotiators from the rest of Canada would probably be subject to strong political pressures not to yield to Quebec's demand that it be treated as an equal partner in future joint institutions to be set up after independence.

Negotiations leading to European integration are being held on a "win-win" basis, with all parties on an equal footing. But renegotiating an economic union between an independent Quebec and ROC would take place in a tense context, likely on a "win-lose" basis. Quebec would have to be prepared to lose its privileged access to several sectors of the Canadian market and also to lose benefits from Canadian trade policies that currently favor Quebec. Why, for example, would ROC guarantee Quebec dairy producers 60 % of the Canadian milk market? Why would ROC continue subsidizing Quebec textile and furniture manufacturers? These current policies are based on relations of mutual trust, and offer something to everyone. But they would have little justification after Quebec independence.

Moreover, the interventionist philosophy of Quebec's current government would lead to the erection of new non-tariff barriers between Quebec and ROC. That in turn would fragment Canada's economic space and bring about a loss of economic surpluses associated with political and economic integration. In fact, the 1993 program of the Parti Québécois calls for a wide range of policies designed to protect and support Quebec companies. If an independent Quebec went ahead with these policies, the rest of Canada might well retaliate, which would make it very difficult to eliminate existing non-tariff barriers.

An analysis of other foreign countries that have split up shows that relations between the two parties after the divorce were marked by distrust and bitterness. In the first part of this book, we have seen what kind of problems the Czech Republic and Slovakia experienced, after the two went their separate ways. Another example is furnished by Singapore, which withdrew from the federation of Malaysia in 1965. Before sitting down at the bargaining table, both governments had recognized the importance of keeping a common currency, and thus of reducing economic uncertainty and promoting trade. But in the end, the two partners were unable to negotiate a monetary union. Indeed, negotiations took place in a climate of distrust and failed for that reason. The two countries never succeeded in agreeing on their respective roles in a central bank. While Singapore demanded a significant role in running the bank, the federation of Malaysia was ready only to grant it a formal role. Besides, Singapore was worried that the ambitious military policies of Malaysia would create inflationary pressures on the monetary union. Singapore could not coordinate its economic policies within a monetary union (Royal Bank of Canada, 1992: 37-38).

THE MONETARY CONSEQUENCES OF INDEPENDENCE

After Quebec independence, which currency and what independence in terms of monetary policy?

In an increasingly interdependent world, financial decisions are not exclusively taken at the level of countries and national governments. With the advent of computers, one trillion dollars change hands every day around the world. These money transfers do not respect boundaries. Nevertheless, investors continue to be concerned about the economic, financial and political stability of countries where they invest, and, when in doubt, they can withdraw their money at any time.

If the breakup of the Canadian federation brought about the end of the monetary union, there would probably be a massive withdrawal of foreign investment. The PQ government knows this only too well. In the PQ's 1993 program, in the event of independence, the PQ favors *"maintaining the **status quo ... with respect to the Bank of Canada, currency and any other institution having a significant effect on the monetary stability of the Quebec-Canada territory"* (Parti Québécois, 1994:62). Moreover, in the draft bill on Quebec sovereignty (December

1994), the Parti Québécois government plans to continue using the Canadian dollar.

But there is a debate on this subject. So far the indépendantiste position has been quite confused. Lucien Bouchard and Jacques Parizeau have proposed by turns that an independent Quebec would have a Canadian dollar, an American dollar or a new Quebec dollar.

Monetary balances are fragile. The example of Slovakia, which had to abandon its monetary union with the Czech Republic six weeks after Czechoslovakia broke up, gives us an idea of the interactive forces that come into play.

We will start by asking just what is the monetary *status quo* the PQ seeks to preserve, and what would be an independent Quebec's room for manoeuvre, in choosing the Canadian dollar or other currencies.

The current situation: as a full member in the Canadian monetary union, Quebec increases its influence

The Quebec financial system is integrated in the Canadian financial system, which is considered one of the most effective in the world. Quebec is part of a political union which enables various governments to develop joint economic and monetary policies, and to harmonize legislative and regulatory standards. This cross-Canada harmonization is very important for Quebec, since it facilitates the mobility of capital, production factors, goods and services with the rest of the country (which is Quebec's largest trading partner) and improves the standard of living of the Quebec population.

While there is no precise measure of the advantages of having a single currency in Canada, we can draw some conclusions from the European experience. According to the European Commission, there is a direct link between a monetary union and the standard of living of the population. The commission says that once the European monetary union becomes a reality, the earnings of Europeans will rise by between 5 % and 10 % (European Economy, 1990:75,83).

In Canada, the Canadian political union enables Quebec to have an important say in the elaboration of monetary policies. The Bank of Canada and the Canadian government together establish the country's monetary policy. As a member of the Canadian federation, Quebec influences monetary policy through the political system: when the Minister of Finance develops macro-economic policies together with the governor of the Bank of Canada, the minister has to take a national view, which means taking the interests of each province into account, including the interests of Quebec. It should be noted that the vice-governor of the Bank of Canada is a Quebecker.

Quebec needs to be able to influence the elaboration of monetary policies in order to determine its own economic policies (job creation, deciding whether to encourage savings or consumption, etc.). Without this influence on monetary policies, a country simply loses control of its economic policies.

That is why the current monetary union allows Quebec to fully benefit from open markets in the rest of Canada as well as to bring its influence to bear on the elaboration of monetary policies. As a result, Quebec has greater control over the direction it wants to give to its own economic policies.

If Quebec separates, the choice of currency, as well as an independent Quebec's ability to influence the choice of monetary policies, will be crucial. Indeed, they will be key factors conditioning the "sovereignty" of the new Quebec state, when it develops its own policies. It is important to analyze the monetary consequences of independence.

Quebec independence would reduce the value of the Canadian dollar

Financial markets are by nature stateless and mobile: investors, forever on the lookout for a better return, can instantly decide to sell or to buy assets or currency anywhere in the world. Independence would increase the risk associated with the Canadian dollar, bringing in turn a decline in the value of the

Canadian dollar. In fact, international investors, faced with the possible splintering of the Canadian monetary zone, the increased risk of default of the two governments and political instability, would start selling a significant portion of their Canadian holdings.

What other changes would Quebec independence bring about? Everything depends on the monetary scenario that develops. We will examine seven possible scenarios.

Monetary scenario 1: Quebec uses Canadian currency with Canada's consent, but loses its influence

This scenario is an extension of the *status quo*. However, a change should be noted in the influence that Quebec is able to exert on the monetary policy of the Bank of Canada. As we have already seen, this influence is currently real. Some political scientists even suggest that Quebec's influence on federal decisions is greater than the 25 % share it has of Canada's population. Quebec's political clout is the equivalent of somewhere between 33 % and 50 %, depending on the area under consideration. By virtue of its "distinct" situation within Canada, Quebec has an effective veto power over certain policies. If Quebec became independent, Quebec's clout in a future "reassociation" with the rest of Canada would not be greater than its demographic weight (25 %). It can even be foreseen that Quebec's clout would drop well below the 25 % level.

In other words, the current PQ government's scenario of the *status quo* without a political union will result in a loss of influence for Quebec in its relations with the rest of Canada.

Monetary scenario 2: Quebec uses Canadian currency without Canada's consent, at the cost of significant economic sacrifices

If needed, Quebec could use Canadian currency without asking for Canada's consent. Contrary to what some people think, Canada could not prevent such use being made of the Canadian dollar, just as the United States cannot prevent the Barbados from using the American dollar as its national currency. To reduce this argument *ab adsurdam,* Quebec could also choose the French franc, the German mark or the Japanese yen as its national currency. The countries chosen would certainly be very flattered. But if Quebec chose the German mark, how would it obtain enough German marks? If an independent Quebec chose the French franc, the American dollar or the Japanese yen, where would it get its cash from? The only way to build up cash reserves in a foreign currency is to generate explort surpluses with the country whose currency is being used.

This reasoning can also be applied to the Canadian dollar. Quebec can now obtain Canadian dollars when the Bank of Canada issues money and when Quebec exports to the rest of the country. If Canada rejected any monetary union with an independent Quebec, the latter would only be able to obtain Canadian dollars by exporting to the rest of Canada or by taking in a massive and continuous supply of financial capital. It should be noted that financial flows are much greater nowadays than commercial flows. In order to obtain permanent liquidities in a foreign currency, an independent Quebec either will have to be ultracompetitive (by selling more than it buys), or will have to attract financial capital with appropriate policies.

It is not realistic to suppose that an independent Quebec would be able to maintain large and permanent trade surpluses with the rest of Canada in order to finance its cash requirements - unless the new Quebec state accepted a big price and wage decline. At the same time, an independent Quebec's ability to permanently attract foreign capital is just as improbable.

Using the Canadian dollar without the consent of the rest of Canada therefore seems to be feasible on the very short term but impossible on the mid and long term.

Monetary scenario 3: Quebec uses American currency with the consent of the United States, at the cost of big economic sacrifices and the loss of its "sovereignty"

If the United States agrees to include Quebec in the American monetary zone, Quebec will be able to use the U.S. dollar, but at a high cost. It will be necessary first of all to convert all Quebec assets into American currency at a quite low conversion rate (certainly not one-for-one). Quebec will then have to abandon any idea of monetary independence and will fall permanently under the authority of the Federal Reserve Bank. In turn, the Federal Reserve will decide both how to distribute currency and how to set interest rates for the entire territory under its authority, including Quebec. The end result for Quebec will be to surrender complete sovereignty in this area to the United States.

Monetary scenario 4: Quebec uses American currency without the consent of the United States

In this scenario, we can apply the same analysis as we did earlier in monetary scenario 2. Quebec will have to obtain U.S. dollars by means of trade surpluses. It might be a realistic solution for the Bahamas, where tourism generates trade surpluses and makes the use of the American dollar possible. But this would be unthinkable for Quebec, since it would quickly run out of the cash it needed.

As a result, this scenario has to be abandoned, for the same reasons as scenario 2.

Monetary scenario 5: Quebec uses a Quebec currency pegged to the Canadian dollar, but becomes more dependent than ever

This scenario is much like scenario 1. Quebec creates a local currency that might be called the Quebec dollar. It is pegged to the Canadian dollar. To maintain its currency in fixed parity with the Canadian dollar, Quebec will have to develop a monetary policy in line with that of the Bank of Canada and to adopt the same interest rates.

Once again, Quebec will sacrifice its sovereignty and will be much more dependent than it is today.

Monetary scenario 6: Quebec uses a Quebec currency pegged to the U.S. dollar and loses all "sovereignty"

This scenario is much like scenario 4. The Quebec dollar will be pegged to the U.S. dollar and the Bank of Quebec will dutifully imitate all policies of the Federal Reserve Bank in order to maintain the Quebec dollar in fixed parity with the U.S. dollar. In practice, everything will happen as if Quebec were using an American dollar that only looked different. The image of René Lévesque will grace the Quebec dollar, in the place of Abraham Lincoln, but for all intents and purposes the two currencies will be identical. It should be noted that it is very hard to maintain two currencies in fixed parity without the active cooperation of the two central banks.

But even if the two currencies are maintained in fixed parity, this will amount to a loss of "sovereignty," since the Bank of Quebec will have to follow the lead of the Federal Reserve and not the other way around.

Monetary scenario 7: Quebec will use a floating Quebec currency at the cost of an economic recession

In this last scenario, Quebec creates an independent Quebec currency, and the Bank of Quebec determines its own monetary policy. This is the only scenario worthy of being called "sovereignist," but it is also the most dangerous one for the Quebec economy, since it would lead to higher rates on government bonds, higher real interest rates, and a corresponding drop in private investment expenses.

One can foresee a series of consequences. First of all, interest rates would likely rise. After independence, investors would incorporate a higher risk premium in the loans they made, while slapping higher interest rates both on the Government of Quebec and on companies operating in Quebec. As we have seen above, in myth 4, financial markets would take into account three kinds of risk, in buying Quebec government bonds after independence: the political risk, the risk associated with exchange rates and the risk of default.

Second of all, there is a risk that the solvency rating of an independent Quebec would drop: Quebec's economic outlook would be less promising, since it would no longer receive federal transfers and its receipts would depend entirely on the Quebec economy, which is smaller and less diversified than the Canadian economy and therefore more vulnerable to disruption. The receipts of the Government of Quebec would be less stable in an independent Quebec than they are within the federal system.

Moreover, the solvency of Quebec government bonds would take a hit, since they would no longer be backed up by federal government guarantees: by pooling interprovincial risks, the federal government reduces the risk of default of individual provinces, since the federal government has a larger tax base and thus a more reliable source of revenues than the provinces taken separately. For this reason, the provinces are able to borrow at lower interest rates. By transferring part of their risks to the federal government, the provinces reduce their debt-service costs. This was moreover one of the main reasons that the four original provinces joined together in 1867.

As we have seen above, after Quebec independence the division of the federal debt between Quebec and the rest of Canada will make all debt service more difficult and will increase the risk of default of both parties. Indeed, the revenues of ROC and of Quebec would be supported by smaller tax bases, and would therefore be less reliable than current federal revenues.

We can therefore conclude that the political risk, combined with the risk associated with the exchange rate and the risk of default, would force the Government of Quebec to jack up interest rates on government bonds. Real interest rates would rise as a result, while private investment expenses and national production would both decline. According to the estimate of the Economic Council of Canada, a 100-base-points increase in real interest rates would bring about a permanent loss of some 1.5 % of the long-term GDP of the Canadian common market (Economic Council of Canada, 1991:85-86).

FISCAL QUESTIONS

After Quebec independence: a likely rise in the cost of government services and in taxes

The cost of government services would rise after independence, bringing about an increase in the tax burden of Quebeckers.

As we have already seen in myth 3, the cost of government services would increase, since Quebec would lose all the advantages that come with being a part of the federal system: the economies of scale linked to the production of certain goods and services at the federal level, the system of equalization payments, and the very existence of a federal government, which permits the provinces to pool their risks.

Economies of scale are created by the production of certain goods and services at the federal level (embassies, national defence, airports, postal service, currency, satellites, railways, etc.) and by sharing the general costs of certain services, which brings down the cost of goods and services for individuals. In addition, the federal system of equalization payments, of which Quebec is a net beneficiary, enables the "have-not" provinces (Maritime provinces, Manitoba, Saskatchewan and Quebec) to offer the same quality of basic services as the "have" provinces (British Columbia, Alberta and Ontario).

Besides, the federal government has its own tax base and provides goods and services in the public sector across Canada. This enables the provinces to reduce interest payments on their debt. By separating, Quebec would lose the advantage of economies of scale and of the federal equalization-payment system.

Such a situation would increase the cost of government services in Quebec. The Government of Quebec would have to choose between further borrowing, increasing its debt load, cutting expenses and diminishing the quality of its services, or increasing taxes in order to maintain the same quality of services.

114

Taxes would probably rise after independence

It is highly likely that taxes would increase in an independent Quebec, since its tax base would shrink at the same time as it was forced to take on a higher level of indebtedness. Independence and the resulting uncertainty would probably lead to the departure of a significant chunk of Quebec's tax base, whether because of the migration of individuals or of companies, such as Canadian companies with head offices in Montreal (Air Canada, Canadian National, Canadian Pacific, etc.) For their part, immigrants would find Quebec less attractive, and would be tempted to settle in the anglophone part of North America. During the pre-referendum period ranging from 1979 to 1981, Quebec experienced a net loss of 391 head offices of companies of all sizes. It is interesting to note than after the referendum, in 1981, the number of companies settling in Quebec started to increase, while departures declined. In addition, international and interprovincial net emigration from Quebec reached a high-point during the first term of office of the Parti Québécois, between 1976 and 1981. After 1981, the trend of net emigration slowed down and even reversed during the 1986-1989 period (Raynauld, 1990: 26-27).

Besides, as we have seen in myth 4, once the debt is divided, Quebec will find itself carrying an additional debt load. Quebec would be cut off from Canada's financing engine. In order to expand the market of Quebec government bonds, Quebec would have to finance its new debt by offering preferential interest rates, by cutting expenses and by increasing taxes. Since the tax base would shrink after independence, taxes would rise both for those individuals and companies remaining in Quebec, in order to finance Quebec's debt and maintain the quality of government services.

CONCLUSION: NOTHING IS "IN THE BAG"...
INDEPENDENCE IS A WHOLE NEW BALLGAME

After Quebec independence, it would be a whole new ballgame for such matters as the economic and monetary union, taxation, the common market and even the free-trade zone between Quebec and Canada. In most cases, Quebec will have to start over from scratch in highly unfavorable negotiating conditions, since its 25 % of Canada's population means Quebec needs the rest of Canada more than ROC needs Quebec. NAFTA has created economic flows to Mexico and the United States, making it even less probable that a Canada-Quebec trade agreement could be renegotiated, with the same terms and conditions that Quebec enjoyed before separation.

While it is possible that Quebec could negotiate a "reassociation" with the rest of Canada, it wouldn't be able to do so to its best advantage. Quebec has proportionately greater clout within the Canadian political union than either its share of Canada's population or GDP. But from a negotiating stance outside of this union, Quebec would obtain much less than it currently does, and it would lose influence in all sectors of the Canadian economic union. At best, the Canada-Quebec economic space after the "divorce" would look like a partial free-trade zone, without visible tariff barriers but with many hidden barriers. Economic relations between Quebec and Canada after independence will not be closer than those of Quebec and the United States within NAFTA.

Quebec will lose much of its influence through an eventual economic "reassociation" with Canada, and will become more dependent both on Canada and on the United States. Indeed, whatever monetary scenario an independent Quebec chose, it would suffer a significant loss of "sovereignty." The best way for Quebec to maintain its influence and the competitive position of its companies is to maintain and strengthen the Canadian economic union. This is the only way that Quebec can really hope to be "sovereign," and to improve the standard of living of Quebeckers.

Myth 6: GETTING INTO NAFTA WILL BE A CINCH FOR QUEBEC

Context

The Parti Québécois and the Bloc Québécois both tell us that Quebec could easily remain a full member of the Free Trade Agreement (FTA) and the North American Free Trade Agreement (NAFTA). It is very important for the two parties to reassure the public and the business community that everything will continue as usual after independence and that Quebec's place in the free-trade agreements and the Canadian economic union will not change.

Even more important, by demonstrating that Quebec's membership in the free-trade agreements will be automatic, indépendantistes are trying to prove that Quebec will remain open to the world, no matter what happens. When opponents of independence claim that Quebec would only be shutting itself off from the rest of the world, the best response that indépendantistes can make is to point to the membership of the new Quebec state in the FTA and in NAFTA. Traditionally, the Parti Québécois has always been a fervent supporter of free trade. The Parizeau government claims that since Chile will soon be in a position to join NAFTA, then Quebec cannot be excluded.

It is probable that Quebec will get back into both the FTA and NAFTA, but it won't happen automatically. Everything will have to be renegotiated, by a Quebec whose bargaining power will be weakened. Indeed, Quebec runs the risk of losing crucial acquired rights that it needs both for the survival of its culture and for certain industries.

An independent Quebec could not automatically join the FTA or NAFTA, and would have to renegotiate both treaties

An independent Quebec could not join the FTA and NAFTA without encountering problems, since these treaties do not automatically apply to Quebec. The FTA was signed in 1987, by two sovereign states with well-defined territories, the United States and Canada. NAFTA was signed in 1994 and currently comprises three countries, Canada, the United States and Mexico. There are many indications that this free-trade zone will be extended in the future to include other Latin American countries.

But the breakup of Canada would invalidate the agreement with respect to Quebec and possibly even with respect to Canada (although as we will see, the latter possibility is remote). Indeed, an independent Quebec would not be bound by the international multilateral agreements Canada has signed. An independent Quebec could seek to join the treaties with the consent of all parties, but one of those parties might object. In the case of the FTA and NAFTA, the United States could request that the treaty be renegotiated on the basis of the *rebus sic stantibus* doctrine, according to which a treaty remains in effect, as long as the fundamental conditions under which it was negotiated have not changed. If however there has been a substantial change in conditions (*rebus non sic stantibus*), the whole treaty can then be called into question. The breakup of Canada following Quebec independence would constitute a fundamental change of circumstances that would raise questions about Quebec's part in the agreement, and perhaps even about Canada's part. But while Quebec would have to renegotiate its membership, the rest of Canada could invoke the principal of legal continuity, and designate itself the "successor state to Canada" to keep its part in the treaty intact.

In addition, in the case of the GATT, Quebec could ask to become a member if it were sponsored by Canada, or if it had the consent of two-thirds of the member-states in the GATT.

In recent history, several cases illustrate this situation. When the Soviet Union broke up into several independent republics, both the parties concerned and the international community agreed that the legal continuity of the former Soviet Union (international agreements, diplomatic representation) would be maintained by the Russian Federation under the direction of President Yeltsin. As a result, Russia occupied the former USSR's seat on the United Nations Security Council, and accepted legal reponsibility for disarmament treaties, etc. Ukraine, meanwhile, was required to renegotiate certain treaties, even though it had involontarily become a nuclear power (Ukraine had inherited part of the Soviet nuclear arsenal deployed on its territory). As for the other republics, the problem was solved case by case: they were sometimes bound by agreements signed by the former Soviet Union, and sometimes were required to renegotiate. As a result, with the exception of Russia, which alone was unanimously designated the "successor state to the USSR," nothing was automatic for the other states. Another example is provided by the former Czechoslovakia. After the country broke up into two parts, the Czech Republic and Slovakia, the problem of legal continuity was even more acute than it had been in the USSR, where the dominant position of Russia was never called into question. Czechoslovakia's two successor states had to renegotiate most agreements, although the support of the international community facilitated the renegotiation process.

In the event that Quebec became independent, it is highly likely that the rest of Canada, which has the greater part of the Canadian populaton as well as nine of its ten provinces, would be designated the "successor state" to Canada. It would probably be able to keep the same name, the same institutions and the same Constitution. The Americans and the Mexicans would doubtless accept to renew NAFTA with the rest of Canada, as is and without any changes. But the same rule would not apply to Quebec, which would have to renegotiate its entry into the FTA and NAFTA, once its independence was declared and accepted both by ROC and the international community.

Indeed, the FTA and NAFTA are long and complex documents that took many years of arduous negotiation to thrash out. Satisfying each of the parties required arbitration and tradeoffs, as well as the introduction of particular conditions and exceptions. In Canada's case, a certain number of clauses were inserted in order to protect the country's economy and culture.

We do not want to delve too deeply into this question, since it is beyond the scope of our study to do so. But we will underline three areas where the loss of acquired rights would have a damaging effect on Quebec: first the Auto Pact, then the interventionist policies of the Quebec government, and finally Quebec's geopolitical position.

Quebec would lose advantages it currently enjoys: the Auto Pact

Without the "Auto Pact," negotiated well before NAFTA but enshrined in Chapter 10 of the FTA, the Canadian automobile industry would never have been able to develop the way it has. The pact guarantees sectoral free trade, so that across North America the automobile industry is vertically integrated. Canadian subsidiaries of huge American companies can take on world product mandates for certain models; they also have guaranteed markets for the components of other models.

In 1994, the automobile industry was the most important industry in the Canadian manufacturing sector, amounting to 18.5 % of the total value of Canadian manufacturing deliveries (Statistics Canada, 1994:-5). This industry makes up an important part of Quebec-Ontario exchanges. It represents 24.3 % of Ontario's total manufacturing output (Statistics Canada, 1990:115, 140-151). In 1994, according to the Quebec Ministry of Industry and Commerce, this sector accounted for 23,000 permanent jobs in Quebec. It is also one of the most sensitive sectors, in terms of trade disputes with the United States.

But in North America, the rules of the game have changed since the Auto Pact was signed in 1965. In the 1990s, the transnational mobility of corporations militates against current industrial localizations. By offering cheap labor and privileged access to American consumers, Mexico is able to attract automobile manufacturers. It should be noted that since Mexico's entry into NAFTA, the entire country is becoming a "maquiladora;" with the devalution of the peso, Mexican labor is even cheaper, and production costs have dropped by 40 % as a result. Many companies such as Mercedes-Benz now have assembly plants in Mexico. For this reason, it would be hard to negotiate the Canada-United States Auto Pact in the 1990s. If it had to be negotiated from scratch, the Americans and Mexicans would probably insist on the complete liberalization of exchanges, without either restrictions or guarantees. If the current pact were renegotiated in the future, some parts of it would be subject to debate.

The United Auto Workers, the American automobile union, is opposed to clauses that protect production in Canada, but not to similar protections in the United States. In the event the industry began pulling up roots and moving to Mexico, why should Canadian plants be protected rather than American corporations? The Americans are increasingly challenging the Canadian view that the insurance clauses are permanent.

American automobile companies take the same position. Faced with overcapacity, they are opposed to specific localization safeguards. If General Motors decided to transfer its plants to Mexico, then it would want to have the freedom to transfer not just its Michigan plants, but also its Canadian plants.

In joining the FTA and NAFTA, an independent Quebec would have to abandon its policy of intervening in favor of Quebec companies

Ever since the Quiet Revolution of the 1960s, Quebec has used an industrial strategy inspired by the 17th-century French statesman Jean Baptiste Colbert as well as by Japan's principles of competitiveness. This stratregy, commonly called "Quebec Inc.", consists mainly of creating competitive advantages by coordinating the actions of the Quebec government and business. The Japanese public and private sector work together under the direction of the MITI (Ministry of International Trade), as a way of penetrating foreign markets (a process sometimes referred to as "Japan Inc."). In much the same way, successive governments in Quebec, whether Union Nationale, Liberal or Parti Québécois, have developed pro-active policies to help Quebec companies become more competitive.

During Robert Bourassa's first term in office, the government played the energy card with the James Bay hydroelectric development. When the PQ came to power in 1976, it sought to bring about a "technological and entrepreneurial shift," by means of subsidy programs for companies, tax credits and sales-tax exemptions, in order to promote Quebec industry. Once the provincial Liberals returned to power, they maintained these policies, modernizing them in turn by introducing the concept of industrial clusters, etc. There is now a wide variety of organizations, instruments and policies designed to support Quebec industry and give it a lead over foreign competitors. These policies have thrown up barriers to interprovincial trade and have thus hindered free trade within Canada. But on the whole, they seem to have been justified by some clear-cut successes.

Whereas most of these policies can be accepted or at least tolerated within the context of a federation, they run headlong into dispositions of NAFTA and the GATT. These two latter agreements are designed to reduce the action of governments to a strict minimum, and to eliminate all trade barriers, including those resulting from subtle protectionist policies. The interventionist approach taken by France and Japan is also favored by Quebec and particularly by the Parti Québécois. The Quebec government, acting within the Canadian federation, can develop policies supporting "Quebec Inc." with all impunity - since the Quebec government is not a signatory to international agreements. But if Quebec became independent and signed these treaties, then it would have to abandon interventionist policies that are forbidden by the treaties. A few examples can be given:

National treatment: the FTA stipulates that national governments have to treat imported goods in the same way they treat national goods. An independent Quebec that signed the FTA would have to eliminate several trade barriers currently used by the Quebec government to protect and promote Quebec companies.

Government purchases: Quebec would not be allowed to maintain its preferential buy-Quebec procurement policy (in favor of Quebec companies).

Industrial subsidies: some Quebec government subsidies granted to Quebec companies via the Société générale de financement or other state agencies would not be allowed under the FTA.

Financial institutions: the Free Trade Agreement places very few restrictions on provincial governments when it comes to financial institutions. Article 1703 exempts American residents from the 10/25 rule, which is designed to protect Canadian ownership of financial institutions. But it only applies to financial institutions with a federal charter, not to those with provincial charters, such as the Caisse Populaire. Under the FTA, the Americans got national treatment in this area, which enables them to buy federal financial institutions but not provincial ones. In a new Quebec-United States agreement, however, article 1703 would probably apply to Quebec financial institutions, which are currently one of the most important instruments of Quebec Inc. and guarantee that economic control remains in Quebec hands (Courchene, 1991:32).

It follows from these observations that a declaration of independence would not really increase Quebec's room for manoeuvre within the FTA and NAFTA. On the contrary, independence would reduce Quebec's "sovereignty" as well as its ability to control its own economy. As a Canadian province, Quebec has more room for manoeuvre to maintain protectionist policies that support Quebec companies than it would as an independent country and signatory of international trade agreements.

A separate Quebec would lose bargaining power by weakening its geopolitical position in North America

The strengths and weaknesses of a country sitting at the bargaining table show up very clearly in the agreement that is ultimately struck. International negotiations are not altruistic exercises; instead they are power struggles, in which the weakest gains the least and the strongest gets the lion's share. A question worth asking is: what bargaining power would an independent Quebec have in future NAFTA negotiations?

In the Canada-United States Free Trade Agreement of 1988, Quebec was represented by the Canadian federal government, and had a great deal of clout in that government, because of the large number of Tory MPs from Quebec. Brian Mulroney's Conservative majority in the House of Commons depended on strong Quebec representation. The Prime Minister of Canada was a Quebecker (as indeed all prime ministers of the country have been since 1968, if one excludes the brief interludes of Joe Clark, John Turner and Kim Campbell). If the Conservatives had to curry favor to Quebec, it was not so much for sentimental reasons as for electoral reasons. Quebec had clearly shown its support for free trade with the United States. Adopting the same position helped the Conservatives win the 1988 election, while John Turner's Liberals, who were against free trade, went down to defeat.

In 1990-93, during the negotiation of NAFTA in its current form, the governments of Brian Mulroney, Kim Campbell and Jean Chrétien did everything they could to meet the demands of Quebec, which once again was enthusiastically pushing for a greater liberalization of trade. As a result, Canada strove to shield culture from the effects of free trade, to renew the protections and safeguards contained in the Free Trade Agreement of 1988, and to establish conflict-resolution mechanisms to prevent a protectionist American Congress from slapping punitive tariffs on Canadian and Quebec products. These protections were obtained after bitter discussions, since the United States has immense bargaining power, due to the size of its economy (ten times the size of Canada's), its high level of development and its central geographic location. If Canada had refused to join NAFTA, the United States would have found itself in the enviable position of signing two separate free-trade agreements with Mexico and Canada. If that had been the case, any company wanting to do business in the three countires would have sought to locate first of all in the United States. And the United States would have become the all-important economic player at the centre, in a position to strip its two neighbors of their production factors.

If Canada, a country of 29 million inhabitants occupying half a continent and constituting the world's 7th economic power, had a hard time negotiating a satisfactory trade agreement with its big southern neighbor, then what would an independent Quebec's bargaining power be?

First of all, an independent Quebec would by far be the smallest player. Quebec's 7 million inhabitants would be outnumbered by 22 million Canadians, 88 million Mexicans and 260 million Americans. The United States may be 10 times bigger than Canada. But it is 40 times bigger than Quebec. In demographic terms, French, Quebec's official language, would be in fifth or sixth spot on the continent, after English, Spanish and perhaps Chinese and Japanese which are increasingly being used in the western part of the continent. If Quebec refused to join NAFTA and negotiated a sort of common market with the rest of Canada, foreign corporations would still be able to break into the Quebec market via Ontario and New Brunswick. Quebec's refusal to be part of NAFTA would not frighten anyone, since its markets would still be accessible thanks to an even partial economic union with the rest of Canada. In other words, Quebec's position at the bargaining table would be to seek favorable conditions, not to demand them.

Second of all, if Quebec becomes independent, its geographic position will prove to be a weakness more than a strength. Without an opening on the Pacific, Quebec will have reduced access to big Asian markets and to the free-trade zone shaping up in the Asia-Pacific region. Moreover, Quebec will have to double its efforts to remain competitive, since it is tucked away in the northeast part of the continent, at a time when economic activity is increasingly moving south and southwest (see myth 8 below). Quebec is located in the "snow belt," known for its harsh winters, and thus seems less attractive for high-technology companies that are flocking to the "sun belts" of Europe and America alike. Quebec has a better chance of making up for these geographic handicaps by remaining a part of Canada, since that enables Quebec to keep its window on the Pacific, and to continue benefiting from equalization payments, labor mobility, and the economic expansion of the West coast.

Third of all, it should be noted that the eventual expansion of NAFTA would increase the number of players and thus dilute Quebec's bargaining power still further. At the end of 1994, President Clinton described his vision of a free-trade zone stretching across both North and South America, from Alaska to Argentina. Quebec has formed an alliance with anglophone provinces in Canada that are willing to accomodate it. By building on this alliance and negotiating through Canada, Quebec can bolster its own negotiating position, as NAFTA gradually expands to include new members.

We have already seen that it is not always easy for a big country like Canada to have its way in international negotiations involving demographic and commercial giants. It is reasonable to suppose that negotiations would be even more difficult for a small country like Quebec after independence. It is sometimes said that Quebec could forge alliances with its "Latin cousins" against the Anglo Saxons. This argument unfortunately does not hold water, since in trade matters, economic considerations take precedence over cultural ones. If Mexico sees a chance of making off with automobile assembly plants currently located in Quebec, arguments about Latin culture are going to make absolutely no difference. As paradoxical as it may seem to indépendantistes, Quebec has two natural allies in NAFTA: the rest of Canada and above all Ontario. Quebec's best chance of maximizing its advantages at the negotiating table is to form a common front with other provinces within Canada.

CONCLUSION: EVERYTHING WILL HAVE TO BE RENEGOTIATED, BUT QUEBEC WILL BE IN THE POSITION OF "SEEKER"

It seems probable that the new state of Quebec would have to renegotiate its entry into free-trade agreements with the United States, Canada and Mexico. Of course, advocates of independence can take heart in the likelihood that Quebec could join these treaties.

But clearly, Quebec's bargaining power at the negotiating table will be almost nil, since Quebec would suffer more from not being a party to the treaties than other countries would suffer from its absence. Other countries could break into Quebec markets via Canada in any case.

Quebec would thus be a "seeker" and would have to accept conditions imposed by its partners. Unless the partners demonstrate a rare degree of altruism at the negotiating table, Quebec would end up losing advantages that Canada has already negotiated, such as cultural exemptions. The "cultural solidarity" proclaimed by Bernard Landry, that supposedly binds those countries wishing to protect their culture, will not be to Quebec's advantage (debate in the National Assembly, Dec. 19, 1994). Hispanic culture is the second-strongest culture in the Americas. The solidarity to protect culture will be among Spanish-speaking countries alone. To each his own!

Myth 7: QUEBEC WILL BE MORE COMPETITIVE AS AN INDEPENDENT COUNTRY THAN IF ITS STAYS IN THE CANADIAN FEDERATION

Context

If Canada is really preventing Quebec from fulfilling its potential, the way we so often hear, does that mean an independent Quebec would be more competitive? There is a lot at stake, since a loss of competitiveness in this era of globalization results in a drop in revenue, negative multiplier effects and less employment. An independent Quebec will therefore have to do everything it can to keep and attract mobile corporations, which can relocate quickly to places where costs are lower and profits higher, thanks to the high transnational mobility of production factors.

Regional or national competitiveness strategies are based nowadays on competitive advantages, whether natural or artifical, that favor an industrial location. The opposite of the competitive advantage is the competitive handicap (Valaskakis, 1992).

Among competitive advantages and handicaps of natural origin are the geographic location of a country (central of peripheral, Northern or Southern, maritime or continental), its climate, surface and sub-surface resources, etc. In the private sector, advantages include infrastructure, the availability and quality of human resources, economies of scale derived from the presence of companies and consumers, etc. Disadvantages can include pollution, overcrowding, crime rates, etc.

But it is at the level of government policy that one finds those variables that most often affect business-location decisions: tax and monetary policies, the investment climate, the presence or absence of industrial subsidies, tax levels, etc. Governments have the power to create advantages by means of intelligent policies, or to create competitive handicaps by means of ill-conceived policies.

An independent Quebec will therefore have to face the challenge of remaining competitive on the international scene. But in a competitive world consisting not just of Ontario and the Northeastern United States, but also of the Pacific coast and Mexico, how will Quebec attract and hold on to production factors and mobile corporations on the long term? How will Quebec be more competitive outside of the Canadian federation?

This question is certainly a complex one and we will address it at several different levels. Quebec is definitely much more attractive for companies as a member of the Canadian federation, than it would be as a separate state: the economic, political and social uncertainty brought on by independence, combined with tax increases, a high level of debt and more unemployment, might well keep companies away, at least for a time. So much for companies that haven't set up shop here yet. Quebec would also run the risk of massively losing companies already established here, and it is only once the breach was closed that an independent Quebec could begin planning new policies to attract new companies here. But since an independent Quebec would not really be "sovereign," it is unlikely it would have the room for manoeuvre it needed to act as it saw fit.

THE CURRENT SITUATION IN QUEBEC: DESPITE AN ADVANCED INDUSTRIAL STRUCTURE CREATED BY THE COMBINED EFFORTS OF PROVINCIAL AND FEDERAL GOVERNMENTS, QUEBEC IS ALREADY FACING CHALLENGES IN IMPROVING ITS COMPETITIVENESS

Quebec within Canada has benefited from "nationalist" Canadian policies, designed to neutralize the power of attraction of regional competitors

The huge American market at Canada's door has always exerted a power of attraction on companies. With the emergence of other middle powers on the American continent, Canada has to battle hard to maintain its competitive position. From the time of John A. MacDonald up to Pierre Trudeau, Canada has developed aggressive industrial policies, which have benefited Quebec in particular. In the early years of Confederation, the "national policy" led to the development of Canada's transportation infrastructure: transcontinental rail lines were built, and sufficiently high customs tariffs were imposed that it was in the interest of foreign companies to settle in Canada to serve the Canadian market. This policy lasted in one form or another until the end of the Trudeau era, and was illustrated in the 1970s, for example, by the active role of the State in setting up regional development projects. Successive governments of Quebec followed on the heels of the federal government. To cite the best-known example, Quebec Inc. is made up of a network of private-sector companies, sponsored and sometimes subsidized by the State. Quebec's competitiveness has also been strengthened by federal subsidies.

Quebec would not have such an advanced industrial structure nowadays, had it not been for the the combined efforts of the federal and Quebec governments. The natural flows of the North American economy would have favored an industrial location well to the south of the Quebec-Ontario corridor.

Even without independence, Quebec is threatened with progressive de-industrialization.

It is true that Quebec has acquired a modern industrial structure over the last thirty years. But that structure leaves a lot to be desired. In fact, up until the early 1990s, the model of industrial incubators was followed rather than that of industrial clusters (namely, bringing companies together under an umbrella, so they can exchange information, create strategic alliances, sometimes merge their operations and take on foreign markets together). This strategy has helped Quebec chalk up a few points but has not turned Quebec into an industrial power the way people had hoped.

Several studies show that current-day Quebec suffers from weaker productivity and a less competitive economy than the Canadian economy taken as a whole. Its productivity is little better than average, and resulted in a scarcity of job offers (only 7,000 jobs created in 1993), due to the inability of the private sector to actively take part in economic recovery (D.G. nord-sud, 1991). From 1988 to 1992, there was a net loss of manufacturing jobs, partly because of the large proportion of low value-added activities (38.2 % of the manufacturing sector in 1986, compared to 20 % for Ontario). Those activities are very vulnerable to the effects of international competitition and are generally uncompetitive in free-trade situations.

A threat hangs over Quebec, as well as over Ontario, with or without independence: progressive de-industrialization, due to the departure of industries and companies to other, more attractive countries. Some companies set up their subsidiaries or even their head offices in countries that ensure access to large markets. Many companies that are currently big stars in the Canadian corporate world, such as Northern Telecom and Bombardier, find the central position of the United States at the heart of NAFTA very attractive. Other companies are trying to keep labor costs to a minimum, and are attracted by countries such as Mexico, which offer low labor costs on the doorstep of the huge consumer market of the United States.

Clearly, it would be much easier for Quebec to improve its competitive position in the international market by remaining a part of Canada, than by heading out on its own. The power of attraction exerted by the United States and Mexico on Canadian companies can only be resisted within a large grouping like Canada.

THE POTENTIAL IMPACT OF SOVEREIGNTY ON QUEBEC'S COMPETITIVENESS

An independent Quebec will have a hard time attracting foreign companies and investors

The worst possible handicap for an independent Quebec would be the perception of foreign investors that it was a "marginalized" country. With 7 million consumers, the domestic market of Quebec would be too small to attract large industries. The localization of foreign companies in Quebec will depend on Quebec's ability to demonstrate it is a gateway to the North American free-trade zone, and more attractive than the United States and Mexico. Quebec will therefore have to put in place fiscal policies that are more generous than those in place in the United States, as well as very competitive salaries that would probably require a devaluation of Quebec currency, if there was one.

The new republic of Quebec will have the entire burden of proof to "sell" its advantages to demanding investors, who would likely find the rest of Canada, the United States and Mexico more attractive. The new republic would have to forget about its social-security and cultural projects, as laid out in the Parti Québécois platform, as well as protectionist policies that violate international agreements such as the FTA, NAFTA and the GATT. The Quebec government will have a hard time proving it can do better after independence. The challenges facing it will be immense!

An uncertain future for the Montreal region, a big industrial centre

The question of the competitive future of the (metropolitan) Montreal region is extremely important for Quebec, since 45 % of the province's population and 47 % of its jobs are concentrated there. Three-fourths of these jobs are in the service sector, an important engine of growth, but the region also accounts for half of Quebec's manufacturing activity, and two-thirds of Quebec's international exports ($8 billion a year) pass through the port of Montreal. The region has the following assets:

- A privileged geographic location, at the hub of several transportation and communications networks, and close to the American market.

- A diversified economic structure, although manufacturing activity remains largely specialized in low value-added activities.

- The existence of a large reserve of qualified and experienced manpower.

- The presence of a large service sector

- A vast network of public health and educational establishments, including four universities.

- The presence of two strategic high-value-added industries: aersopace (40 % Canadian production, $3 billion of deliveries, 30,000 jobs and 70 % of production headed for export) and the pharmaceutical industry (36 % of the jobs in this sector in Canada, $250 million in public and private research and development investments).

The public sector accounts for one-fourth of direct employment on the island of Montreal, since the various public administrations have their offices on the island. But that figure does not include the island's many health and educational establishments, or paragovernmental agencies. In 1987, according to a study of the OPDQ, the metropolitan region of Montreal (Montreal Urban Community or MUC, and Laval) had:

- 169 federal-government establishments, offering 16,000 direct jobs.

- 190 provincial-government establishments, employing 17,000 people, without counting the MUC's 30 municipalities.

- A vast educational network, bringing together 9 university establishments, 11 CEGEPS (junior colleges),and 565 elementary and secondary schools.

- Commercial and industrial activity (construction starts, retail trade, industrial activities) amounted to $5.5 billion in 1989.

An important question is whether private investors will find Montreal a more attractive city in a country with a market of 29 million people or as the metropolis of a new country with 7 million inhabitants. Will Montreal's economic power of attraction and reputation as an international city be increased by Quebec independence or not?

Montreal is already losing ground. Among·Canada's large cities, it is the capital of poverty. The economy of Montreal, like that of Toronto, is growing weaker because of the economic recession and the departure of industries to the United States and Mexico. Since the end of the 1970s, Montreal has actually or practically lost the head offices of large Canadian multinationals, such as Sun Life, Royal Trust, Northern Telecom, the Royal Bank, the Bank of Montreal... This has resulted in a drop in real-estate prices and a low rate of construction of new office buildings and residential homes. The independence of Quebec would only aggravate this decline, unless Montreal were to become the new capital of the republic, which scarcely seems likely, given the fact Premier Jacques Parizeau has established his official residence in Quebec and has promised to make it the national capital.

Quebec independence would have the following probable consequences:

The future separation of Quebec would accelerate the decline of the metropolitan region of Montreal

(1) There would be a massive departure of companies.

Many Canadian corporations, such as financial institutions, insurance companies, Canadian National, Canadian Pacific, Air Canada, Bell Canada, would leave Montreal, while maintaining an office in the city.

Some multinationals, whose head offices are currently located in the Montreal region, might wish to leave because of the climate of political and monetary instability and the rise in interest rates. So would some high-tech firms, deprived of research and developement subsidies ($500 million of which comes directly from the federal government).

(2) The elimination of most of the federal civil service's 16,000 jobs in Montreal would have a negative multiplier effect on the region's economy some three times higher than the 16,000 figure would suggest.

(3) Quebec would pick up whatever Montreal lost in terms of employment in the provincial civil service, since Quebec is supposed to become the most important focus of development and the national capital of Quebec. This could lead to the transfer of services and bureaucrats to Quebec City, and to the possible departure of consulates of small countries that would have to leave Montreal, or reduce their representation.

Montreal's decline could be checked, however, if the new government of an independent Quebec decided to make it the capital of the country. In this case, Montreal would become a big international capital and, would have added status in the view of the international élite. This improvement in Montreal's fortunes would be detrimental to the rest of Quebec, and would therefore be politically unacceptable to the Parti Québécois, which favors a bipolar state, with two growth centres, Quebec City and Montreal.

An uncertain future for the regions of an independent Quebec, some of which have developed thanks to the combined actions of the federal and Quebec governments

For more than 35 years in Canada, on the federal as much as on the provincial level, regional development has been a way of developing greater social equity and more harmonious development in non-urban centres. In Quebec, the federal and provincial governments have always played a key role. One of the purposes of regional development is to encourage the growth of employment in distant and poor regions. That is why some regions, such as the Lower St. Lawrence, receive more from the government than other regions do.

As a result, governments have taken measures along these lines and developed policies with a view to stimulating the different regions by making up for unequal growth. Subsidy programs have been set up, for locating companies in designated regions, and tax incentives have been created. Many studies have been conducted, commissions of inquiry set up, and ministries and public organizations created, among them the Department of Regional Economic Expansion (1970). the Office de la planification et du développement du Québec (1968), etc. More recently, in 1984, we saw numerous government policies established, to promote better regional development. Some of these policies have been the result of cooperation between the two levels of government (the Canada-Quebec auxiliary agreement on regional development and the Canada-Quebec agreement on manpower training, etc.).

An assessment of the steps taken to promote regional development since 1960 shows that there have been problems, but on the whole regional-development policies have been successful. Some Quebec regions, such as the Eastern Townships, the Lower St. Lawrence, the South Shore and Saguenay-Lac St. Jean, have benefited from government actions that helped them develop gradually. In many cases, non-governmental·initiatives, at the local and regional levels, have taken over from regional-development programs. Over the last 20 years, these government initiatives have generated some $15 billion of economic benefits, and have helped maintain 230,000 jobs in Quebec's regions. The number of jobs in all of Quebec rose by 42.1 % between 1971 and 1990, contributing to a big rise in disposable personal income, which rose 60 % across all Quebec regions. Most industrial parks in the regions of Quebec were established thanks to the work of regional policies. The industrial development of the Eastern Townships was launched in the 1960s, through a series of federal and provincial subsidies. Today, this region is proud to have a world leader in microprocessors, C-MAC, and a series of other development poles.

The federal government does not meddle in the administration of funds, and has accepted the concept of progressive decentralization and the delegation of management to the provincial government and to some extent to municipalities via MRCs (municipalités régionales de comté).

After independence, Quebec regions could gradually lose the benefits obtained through 35 years of economic development, since Quebec would be deprived of federal transfers that currently make up some 21.5 % of budget revenues (see the Quebec budget, 1994). Those transfers serve to provide established-program funding and, to some extent, to support regional development.

CONCLUSION: AN INTEGRATED CROSS-CANADA COMPETITIVENESS STRATEGY IS IN QUEBEC'S BEST INTERESTS

Instead of trying to strike out on its own, Quebec should harmonize its development policies and integrate its industrial clusters along with those of Ontario. The fact of the matter is that competitiveness is determined at the level of large regions. It is less a case of Montreal versus Toronto or Quebec against Montreal, than of the Quebec-Windsor corridor (Central Canada) against the Northeastern United States, against the "maqiladoras" and against the Pacific Coast. A well-thought-out strategy of competitiveness for Canada would encompass Quebec and Ontario, which constitute an economic region, even though three governments have jurisdiction over this region. Revitalizing the Quebec-Windsor corridor is essential for the development of Quebec as well as of Ontario.

If it is already difficult, within the Canadian federation, to harmonize the development policies of Quebec and Ontario, it would be pratcially unthinkable to do so after Quebec independence. Economic wars would probably break out between the two provinces, as they each sought to attract foreign investment.

If Ontario adopted an Ontario Inc. approach, along Quebec lines, creating powerful "attractors" to neutralize Quebec's initiatives, then Quebec would be facing an uphill struggle. Ontario would have the stronger hand, since it would have 10 million producer-consumers, without counting those in the rest of Canada, and a greater investment capacity, than 7 million Quebeckers. The interprovincial "attractors" wars will be a boon for stateless corporations, since they will witness a bidding war between Quebec and Ontario, both of which will be upping the ante, in the form of industrial subsidies, in order to attrack investment. In the final analysis, taxpayers will be the ones to pay the hefty ransoms offered to attract investment.

Unless the rest of Canada and Quebec's real competitors suddenly stop competing, there is no reason to suppose that an independent Quebec would be more competitive than Quebec now is as part of Canada. On the contrary, the policy with the best chance of succeeding is a cross-Canada industrial strategy, or at least a Canadian strategy of industrial clusters. The "every man for himself" strategy favored by the Quebec indépendantiste movement rejects the idea of collective initiatives, even when it comes to developing new markets. One has only to recall the absence of the Quebec premier during the trade trip Team Canada made to China n November 1994. In our opinion, this is a huge strategic error running against Quebec's interests.

As a Mexican diplomat told one of the authors a few months ago: *"We just can't understand you Canadians. You accept to wage economic war against the United States and Mexico within NAFTA, without so much as a campaign strategy. Against our 88 million Mexicans and 260 million Americans, you send your 29 million soldiers, one by one, without any kind of team spirit. Thanks for the gift. Rest assured that with that kind of strategy, we are the ones who will conquer your markets, and not the other ay round. Maybe in a few more years, we will be in a position to offer you some development assistance!"*

The words of the Mexican diplomat illustrate all the importance of jointly taking on foreign markets, the way Team Canada did during its China visit in November 1994.

Myth 8: FULL EMPLOYMENT WILL BE EASY TO BRING ABOUT IN AN INDEPENDENT QUEBEC

Context

The program of the Parti Québécois promises that there would be less unemployment in an independent Quebec, thanks to economic-recovery and full-employment policies and the creation of regional development commissions and local employment centres. In addition, there would be policies to influence the active management of employment, by means of assistance and support for Quebec firms that want to get involved in export activities as well as the establishment of objectives for the coordination and content of professional training, etc. However, the Parti Québécois program makes no mention of how such policies would be paid for. Where would an independent Quebec find the means to finance the programs required to bring about full employment?

If one looks at the evolution of employment in Quebec over the last twenty years, it is clear that the unemployment rate in Quebec has always been higher than the North American average (Canadian and American). One of the distinguishing characteristics of the Quebec labor market is the gap between the rise in demand for employment and the offer of new jobs made by companies. At the beginning of the 1970s came a significant rise in the unemployment rate, followed by a worsening of the rate in the mid-1970s, when the Parti Québécois was in power (the rate was 10.3 % and 10.9 % in 1977 and 1978, whereas in Ontario during the same period the rate stood at 7 % and 7.2 %). The same thing happened during the 1981-82 recession (10.3 % and 13.8 % in Quebec, compared to 6.5 % and 9.8 % in Ontario). This situation prevailed even during years of economic growth, for example at the end of the 1980s: in 1989, the unemployment rate in Quebec was 9.3 %, compared to rates in Ontario of 5.1 % and across Canada of

7.5 %. With the start of the 1990s, Quebec's employment situation deteriorated still further. In spite of some economic recovery, the unemployment rate in 1993 was 13.1 %, compared to the national average of 11.2 %.

The Quebec unemployment rate is regularly below the Ontario average in particular and the Canadian average in general. This gap is due to a structural problem, not to the business cycle, and is not only true of Quebec, but also of the Maritime Provinces, which have an even higher unemployment rate. How will an independent Quebec be able to solve this problem? We will first examine the principal causes of unemployment (in Quebec as well as elsewhere) and the real room for manoeuvre the government of an independent Quebec would have to eliminate those causes.

INDEPENDENCE UP AGAINST UNEMPLOYMENT: WHAT IS THE REAL ROOM FOR MANOEUVRE?

To understand the challenges an independent Quebec would face in its quest for full employment, it is important to analyze seven questions which we will lay out before the read in the order of importance: the business cycle, institutional rigidity, monetary policies, budgetary policies, manpower training, technological change, and globalization. In each of these cases, we will examine whether an independent Quebec could apply effective solutions.

1. The business cycle: whether Quebec is independent or not, it will not be able to fight unemployment by increasing government expenditures

Quebec has always been more vulnerable to economic slowdowns than the rest of Canada. Quebec suffered a lot during the recessions of 1980-81 and 1991-92. And although in 1995, the economic recession is officially over, the job market situation remains difficult, particularly in some regions like Montreal. Generally, governments seek to resolve the problem of recession-driven unemployment by increasing government expenses.

The creation of jobs by increasing government expenditure is possible. But it is extremely costly and its indirect negative effects are counter-productive, particularly in an open system. In the current economic situation, increasing government spending is impossible, since it would lead to additional deficits for Quebec. And Quebec cannot increase taxes, without running the risk that mobile companies and executives would move out and consumers would decide to work in the underground economy. In addition, the excessive debt load of the Canadian and Quebec public sectors makes it difficult to take out new loans in order to finance countercyclical government deficits. An independent Quebec will be faced with economic difficulties, and will not be in a position to increase government spending.

2. The "individual" and institutional rigidities that cause unemployment, would grow worse in an independent Quebec

One way to explain the persistance of unemployment, even during a recovery, is the lack of flexibility of the labor market. Quebec manpower is not very mobile: Quebeckers move less than Americans, they don't look for work in other provinces, they prefer their region and even their city. To this "individual" rigidity is added a sort of "institutional rigidity," created by the massive unionization of the public and private sectors.

To a certain extent, it will be possible within an independent Quebec to increase the internal mobility of manpower by means of government policies. But independence will also limit the mobility of Quebec workers seeking work outside of Quebec. In fact, an independent Quebec will not have greater room for manoeuvre to address the institutional causes of unemployment: it will not be able to limit the power of labor unions, which are among the most ardent supporters of independence. Moreover, rolling back the acquired rights of workers, by reducing their salaries or by aggravating work conditions, would be a political and social blunder. We can therefore conclude that an independent Quebec would have very little room for manoeuvre to eliminate the rigidity that causes unemployment.

3. Manpower training: the government of an independent Quebec will not be able to do much more

Over the last 35 years, entrepreneurship has progressed in Quebec. But the weak productivity of Quebec labor and the lack of competitiveness of the Quebec economy compared to the Canadian economy as a whole, puts Quebec at a disadvantage when it faces the new challenges of competition and globalization. According to some studies, the problem is to be found in an inadequate organization of work in Quebec, a labor force that is not as skilled as that of our foreign competitors, and high unitary costs (Interventions économiques, 1988).

What can an indépendantiste government do in this area? As the bureaucrats of an independent Quebec face the turmoil created in the labor market by technological change, are they going to be better qualified than their federal colleagues to start up manpower-training programs? The Europeans are trying to develop standards and programs that are continental in scope, rather than local. The "small is beautiful" model appeals to people who believe in the importance of local initiatives, but that model is not always effective. Quebec already has full sovereignty in the domain of education, since education is a provincial jurisdiction in Canada. But Quebec's education system is relatively mediocre, and the high-school dropout rate is extremely high (in 1994, the dropout rate in the francophone sector of the province's largest board, the Montreal Catholic School Commission, was 46 %). How will independence improve that state of affairs?

4. An independent Quebec will have practically no way to influence the monetary policies that determine its economic policies

The restrictive monetary policies pursued by the federal government between 1988 and 1993 led to high interest rates and an overvalued Canadian dollar, compared to the American dollar. This situation hindered exports and brought on bankruptcies which naturally wiped out jobs. Now, at the beginning of 1995, interest rates in Canada are relatively low, by Canadian standards. However, in real terms (taking inflation into account), these rates are still high compared to American rates. An increase in interest rates, for whatever reason, will have the effect of threatening yet more jobs. In Quebec, the 160,000 small and medium-sized companies account for the jobs of 85 % of the Quebec labor force. Most of these companies depend for their survival on bank financing. If interest rates reached 20 % (the record of the 1990s), many of these companies would have to declare bankruptcy, which would in turn have a catastrophic effect on employment.

To have a hope of changing monetary policy, the new Quebec state would have to have its own currency, in flexible exchange-rate parity with foreign currencies. But as we have seen above in Myth 5, Scenario 7, the cost borne by the Quebec economy would be very heavy: a rise both in interest rates on government securities and in real interest rates, a drop in investments and consumption, etc... Since Quebec would lack monetary sovereignty, interest rates and the value of the Canadian dollar (to be used by Quebec) would be set in Ottawa, without Quebec being consulted or having any real influence. In short, an independent Quebec would have no chance of fighting unemployment by influencing monetary policy.

5. An independent Quebec will not have more room for manoeuvre to reduce unemployment brought about by technological innovations than it currently has.

One of the basic facts of modern life is that innovations in process technologies wipe out jobs by replacing people with machines. At the same time, innovations in product technologies mean that new products are invented, thus creating jobs and generating economic activity. The two most important strategic technological innovations of our time, computers and telecommunications, are horizontal process technologies which can be applied to different sectors of the economy. As a result, the means of production can be modified by increasing efficiency and considerably reducing the demand for manpower.

There is a widening rift between economic growth, fueled by process technological innovations, and job creation.

Our industrialized societies are becoming increasingly productive, but employment tends to shrink. This phenomenon can be found everywhere in the world, and does not affect Quebec alone.

What will the Péquiste government be able to do, in order to face up to this reality? Hold back innovation at the risk of seeing Quebec companies lose their competitive advantages? Distribute productivity gains derived from computers by reducing work hours? In an ideal world, in a closed system, everyone would work less and these rules would apply to all companies. But an independent Quebec would not live isolated from the rest of the world. In an open system, the reduction of work hours without reducing wages results in increased production costs and pressures companies to leave.

6. An independent Quebec will not be able to struggle alone against those effects of globalization that enable companies to locate in countries where manpower is cheaper.

The phenomenon of globalization has an impact on the unemployment rate. The search for "profitability" and "competitiveness" means that companies have a vast range of choices. It is no longer true that "what is good for General Motors is good for Michigan and good for the USA." What is good for GM might be closing plants in Detroit and moving them to Mexico or Hungary. The relocalization of companies and the emigration of industries is one of the causes of unemployment. As long as there is a possibility that factories can be transferred to Third World countries where the labor force is ready (or forced) to work for a pittance, the Stateless Corporation will be able to use this threat to lower wages in industrialized countries and to automate its production lines. Otherwise, it will simply leave. This logic is unassailable and one can hardly blaim the chairman of the corporation, whose responsibility to his shareholders requires him to seek the greatest profit. The success of technologies, coupled with competition from newly-industrialized countries with low wages, is freeing up a growing proportion of the Western labor force, which is often relegated to social welfare, marginalization and poverty. The indépendantiste government of Quebec will not be able to reverse this trend all by itself.

THE OPTIONS AVAILABLE TO THE GOVERNMENT OF AN INDEPENDENT QUEBEC TO BOOST EMPLOYMENT

Given this complex situation, what options are available to the government of an independent Quebec? In our opinion, there are three options:

Option 1: Seek "artificial" full employment in an open system and risk the massive loss of production factors

Option 2: Seek full employment by accepting the impoverishment of the labor force

Option 3: Favor maximum competitiveness without job creation, and find a way to redistribute wealth

Option 1: Seek "artificial" full employment in an open system and risk the massive loss of production factors

Contrary to what some people believe, the objective of full employment can always be reached using artificial methods. If it is decided that employment must become a means of distribution and not of production, then jobs can be created, if need be, for the sole purpose of giving workers purchasing power. To take this argument to absurd heights, the labor force could be divided into two groups the first would work 40 hours a week breaking windows, while the second would work 40 hours a week repairing them! There would be both full employment and full salaries. Whether this example is considered absurd or not, it is a little what happens in wartime. Everyone is occupied at the front or in munitions and supply factories. The more weapons go up in smoke, the more people will have to work to build new ones. When nations wage war, there is no unemployment and everyone is overemployed.

The *windowbreaker/window-repairman strategy* can be applied by a country rich enough to afford it and to function in a closed system. Such a country can even add very generous social security: three months of paid holiday leave per year, a 25-hour work week, complete insurance, etc. So much the better if a country can afford this life of luxury. But the option is not possible for an economy open to international competition. In an open system, the highly generous distribution system would bring about the bankruptcy of local companies, whose manpower costs would become astronomical compared to their foreign competitors, or would cause the departure of these local companies to countries where production costs are lower. And since the open system is likely to be reduced to the lowest common denominator, social security systems will settle at the level of the least generous competitor having the lowest production costs.

The result of the preceding is that an independent Quebec, operating in an open system, will not be able to put in place an artificial full-employment policy, or a generous social policy.

Option 2: Seek full employment by accepting the impoverishment of the labor force

However, it is possible to put in place a policy of full employment by lowering wages and accepting the impoverishment of the labor force. During the Middle Ages, neither slaves nor serfs experienced unemployment. But who wants to be a slave? The social legislation of the last 150 years has lightened the burden of the worker. Is society about to backtrack and return to the excesses of the first industrial revolution? Some people accuse the Americans of doing just that, in order to create jobs in the United States. Real wages in the United States today are lower than they were in 1959. Work conditions are deterioriating, job security doesn't exist and social security leaves a lot to be desired, especially when it comes to health and to those people who have the misfortune of losing their jobs. In some countries, such as the United Kingdom, a true pioneer of social legislation, there is even talk of abolishing the minimum wage. We may ultimately witness what some people are calling the "maquiladorization" of the world economy, in which case work conditions would deteriorate everywhere in order to increase competitiveness. An independent Quebec in an open system will only accelerate this process.

Option 3: Count on maximum competitiveness without job creation, and find the way to redistribute wealth

Quebec will be able to create significant wealth, if it completely abandons the objective of full employment, opts for maximal competitiveness by using cutting-edge technologies and finds the way both to redistribute wealth and to improve the lot of workers without resorting to artificial job creation. But its ability to redistribute wealth will be severely limited by globalization and the openness of its economy. An attempt to redistribute wealth through taxation (for example, by taxing automation) will discourage innovation and encourage the departure of companies and individuals. It is impossible to distribute wealth simply by issuing more money, unless Quebec creates its own currency, which as we have seen above would create more problems than it would solve.

If however Quebec opts for maximum competitiveness without distributing wealth, in one way or another, then it will create a dual economy. This dual economy will be made up of the haves at one end and the have-nots at the other, a situation that could lead to a social revolution or a massive exodus. Support for independence comes above all from those who wrongly believe it will improve their lot in life. When they discover that is not going to be the case, they will revolt.

CONCLUSION: A TOTALLY MADE-IN-QUEBEC POLICY OF FULL EMPLOYMENT ACCOMPANIED BY ADEQUATE SOCIAL SECURITY HAS FEW CHANCES OF SUCCEEDING IN AN OPEN SYSTEM

What general conclusion can we draw concerning the indépendantiste myth of full employment? Given the forces that are brought to bear on the level of employment, the quality of life in the workplace and social security in general, the room for manoeuvre of a government in this respect depends entirely on its will and its ability to fully control its economic space. The phenomenon of globalization and the ever-present possibility that corporations will locate elsewhere indicate that even if a little country of 7 million inhabitants has the will to act, its ability to do so is practically nill. Only large groupings such as the European Union, the United States or China can choose to close themselves off. Quebec cannot seriously imagine becoming a closed economy, unless it accepts the risk of losing ground and leading a marginal existence outside of the world economy. Canada itself, the 7th industrial power in the world and a virtual continent, cannot seriously imagine closing itself off. For Canada as much as for Quebec, the solution to the problems of employment is to be found in international agreements, preferably on a planetary level but at least on a continental level. The problem of employment is now a universal one. That is why the independence of a small country like Quebec, far from changing the situation for the best, will only aggravate it.

Myth 9: THE QUEBEC PEOPLE HAVE THE RIGHT TO SELF-DETERMINATION

Context

Many Quebeckers are confused about the question of Quebec's right to separate, based on the "right to self-determination." They are just as confused about the right of native people to separate and about the borders of an independent Quebec. The confusion about these matters is intentionally perpetuated by Jacques Parizeau and Lucien Bouchard who both claim that the "Quebec people" alone have the right to separate and that the borders of an independent Quebec are inviolable. All these questions seem to be shrouded in fog, creating confusion in the public mind and nourishing the illusion that Quebec's separation will take care of itself, if the people want it, since the Quebec state can create itself by a simple flourish of a magic wand.

In actual fact, the questions relating to territory and self-determination are very delicate. The indépendantistes know that the question of the borders of an independent Quebec will be subject to discussion; the same arguments used by Quebec to "legalize" the process of independence can be used by other minority groups within Quebec. The indépendantistes know that there is a distinct possibility of losing control of the process: on the one hand, the native people might harden their position, the way they have done lately; on the other hand, there might be a hardening among indépendantistes, the way Jacques Brassard, a Parti Québécois member of the National Assembly, called for the use of force, if necessary, to calm rebellious native people after independence; and finally the rest of Canada might toughen its position if it feared for its own future.

We will search for the truth behind this skillfully-perpetuated myth.

QUEBEC HAS NO AUTOMATIC RIGHT TO SEPARATION: THE INTERNATIONAL COMMUNITY ALONE WILL JUDGE WHETHER QUEBEC SEPARATION IS VALID

Canadian law: in Canadian constitutional law, no provision enables Quebec to separate

In Canadian constitutional law, no disposition enables Quebec to separate. In theory at least, an amendment to the Constitution of Canada would be required (Part V of the Constitution Act of 1982) for Quebec to be able to separate legally. This amendment would have to be approved by Ottawa and by all the provinces, even if there exists a tacit consensus that a massive Yes in a clear referendum on the independence of Quebec would constitute the expression of the popular will of Quebeckers.

Some people might wonder whether a Yes victory in a referendum on Quebec independence would push Ottawa and the provinces to unanimously adopt a constitutional amendment allowing the "legal" separation of Quebec. But that scenario is doubtful for several reasons.

First of all, the rest of Canada has a huge interest in this debate: a "prospective" look at the future suggests there would be a grave economic and financial crisis in the rest of Canada (and indeed in Quebec) if Quebec were to separate. Forces to dismember the rest of Canada would likely strengthen. On the short to mid term, Canada would likely splinter into various entitites, some of which might join the United States. How, for example, could the West be prevented from leaving, if Quebec leaves and the rest of Canada is thrown into a serious economic depression?

The Bloc Québécois seems to base part of its program on precisely this prospective view of the future, when it claims that an independent Quebec would be an "unavoidable" partner for the rest of Canada. But that is to forget that any negotiation would be practically impossible if Canada and an independent Quebec floundered in a financial and economic crisis, made worse by emotional passions and the native crisis that could result from the situation. In fact, it is not very likely that the

Prime Minister of Canada and the Premiers of the others provinces would accept to amend the Constitution.

International law: Quebec has no right to separation based on the right to self-determination

In international law, Quebec does not have the right to separate based on the right to self-determination (or the right of peoples to dispose of themselves), since Quebec is neither a colony nor an associated territory. However, nothing in international law prevents Quebec from separating if its population so desires. But in that case it is up to the international community to decide whether or not to validate *de facto* independence, something the international community will or will not do, depending on the circumstances. The balance is therefore delicate. This position was developed in a study on "Quebec's territorial integrity in the event it acceded to sovereignty," drafted by five international legal experts in 1992, at the request of the "Secretary of the commissions on the determination process of Quebec's political and constitutional future," set up under the terms of Bill 150. (Franck et al., 1992). The study talks about Quebec's "right to self-determination," and provides the grounds for a possible challenge by native people to the territory of an independent Quebec.

This study contradicts the conclusions of the Bélanger-Campeau Commission. Even so, Jacques Parizeau and Lucien Bouchard have repeatedly quoted from it. It represents the view of the majority of international legal experts.

The study is often referred to in an incomplete way. A more serious look at the study is needed, if we are to evaluate the real difficulties of the indépendentiste project, on the national and international scene.

According to the five international jurists, Thomas Franck, Rosalyn Higgins, Alain Péllet, Malcolm Shaw and Christian Tomuschat,

"In international law, 'the right of peoples to dispose of themselves' or the 'right to self-determination' does not confer on them the right to accede to independence except

*for 'colonial peoples and those (rare) peoples in compara-
ble situations.'*

*The right to self-determination means above all that 'all
peoples have the right to participate in political, economic,
social and cultural choices involving them.'*

*Quebec lacks the legal grounds to invoke its right to
dispose of itself, since it cannot be "reasonably held that
[Quebec] is a colonial people or that it is deprived of the
right to its own existence in the heart of the Canadian union
and to participate in democratic life."*

Nevertheless, nothing in international law prevents Quebec
from demanding independence and obtaining it. In that case,
independence is a *fait accompli* which the international community will accept or reject.

Independence is only really effective if it receives "rapid"
international recognition from third parties.

There are thus no legal grounds for Quebec independence;
instead there is a *de facto* situation, validated by the establishment
of its own political institutions and the recognition of third parties.

This position is shared by most experts on international law. Two
opinions which could be called "dissident" have been articulated
by the Bélanger-Campeau Commission and Daniel Turp, professor
of international law and an advisor to Lucien Bouchard.

According to these two opinions, the fact that reaching a
significant constitutional reform of Quebec's status within Canada is impossible confers on Quebec a right to separation. Daniel
Turp goes even farther, by saying that the impossibility of reform
must be interpreted as a rejection of Quebec's exercise of its "right
to self-determination" within Canada and therefore authorizes it
to separate, in accordance with international law.

Conclusion: neither international nor Canadian law permits Quebec to unilaterally declare independence

Indépendantistes say that if Ottawa and the provinces do not accept the validity of a referendum on separation, then Quebec would unilaterally proclaim independence:

> *"If Ottawa does not recognize us, we will proclaim our sovereignty ourselves, simply because the entire world will recognize us," said Lucien Bouchard in May 1994 (Robitaille:A-1,A-2).*

If this declaration is analyzed in the light of what we have shown above, then we can conclude that Quebec, in placing itself "outside of the law" in Canada, runs the risk of weakening its international position and of not obtaining the recognition of third parties which is needed for its status as a state to really exist. The legitimacy of a unilateral declaration could however be found in a massive "Yes" of Quebeckers to a clear referendum question on Quebec independence. But given recent developments, this possibility seems more and more remote.

If Quebec independence has no grounds in international law, but becomes a *de facto* situation, then other questions naturally arise.

THE BORDERS OF AN INDEPENDENT QUEBEC ARE NOT UNALTERABLE

The borders of an independent Quebec in its relations with Canada

> *"As long as Quebec stays part of Canada," Prime Minister Jean Chrétien said in May 1994, "no one can change Quebec's borders without the assent of Quebec." Jacques Parizeau and Lucien Bouchard said for their part that the borders of an independent Quebec are the borders Quebec currently has. (Tu Thanh Ha, 1994:A-1, A-2).*

Once independence is confirmed, the protection of Quebec's borders would be based on a principle of international law called the "territorial integrity of states and the stability of borders." This well-established principle has been reiterated on many occasions (Article 2, paragraph 4 of the Charter of the United Nations and by regional organizations such as the Organization of American States in article 12 of its charter). It has also been confirmed by the International Court of Justice. From this point of view, the integrity of Quebec's borders could not be called into question. Federal assets would be transferred to the new state, except for buildings used for purposes of administration and for the federal government, which Canada could continue using as its property.

But if this principle is admitted, it should be noted that nothing could prevent Canada from invoking the same right to the "territorial integrity of states and the stability of borders," which confirms the international legal principle that the right to secession does not exist.

Some people have claimed that the federal government, having ceded the Abitibi to Quebec in 1898 and then the Ungava in 1912, could demand their return. This argument has no validity, since the rules of private law (loan contract) cannot be applied to situations in international law.

One could imagine some regions of Quebec, next to the Ontario boundary, deciding to remain with the rest of Canada.

Quebec is divisible and the native people could use the same process as Quebec to separate and then rejoin Canada

If native people clamored for independence, using the same process as Quebec, the borders of Quebec would be called into question.

Indeed, the native people have no right to separation, based on the right to self-determination, but they can invoke the same rules as those applying to Quebec. Since the independence of Quebec has no basis in international law, but is a *de facto* situation, it would be very difficult for Quebec to deny the accession to independence of native people and, to a less extent, of other minority groups. According to the most common view held by international experts, the native people could, using the same process as Quebec, impose their secession and thus be in a position to rejoin the rest of Canada.

The study cited above on "the integrity of Quebec territory in the hypothesis of the accession to sovereignty" maintains that:

> "it appears prima facie that the rules that can apply to the relations between the Quebec people and Canada apply mutatis mutandi, when it comes to relations between a Quebec having acceded to sovereignty and groups then appearing as its own national minorities."

This opinion is backed up by Daniel Turp, professor of law and advisor to Lucien Bouchard, who writes:

> "The native nations are in a position similar to that of the Québécois when it comes to invoking international law in support of the claim that they have the right to self-determination." (Turp, 1992, 111-118.)

Nothing therefore would stand in the way of various native peoples deciding to create one or more independent states in a sovereign Quebec. These native states could invoke a de facto situation which will have to be recognized by third parties, just as an independent Quebec could. A sovereign Quebec invoking the same principle would be hard-pressed to refuse this right, particularly if native nations decided to remain part of Canada.

This separation within separation would be easier for native people to bring about than for minorities. Unlike the right of "peoples" or "nations," the right of ethnic, linguistic and religious minorities is a modern concept of international law. One can imagine a minority having a well-defined territory. But on the whole, Quebec's minorities are to be found everywhere in Quebec and do not possess a distinct territory, which is a key element in becoming independent. However, if it could be shown that minorities were persecuted in an independent

Quebec, then they could pressure the Quebec government in order to obtain their own autonomy or independence.

As we will see later on, native people are subject to a special regime and international law tends to recognize their wide-spread privileges in terms of territory and ancestral lands. Even though these rights do not include secession, native people occupy tangible territories, allowing them to accede to independence using the same process as Quebec.

DIFFICULTIES CAN BE FORESEEN WHEN IT COMES TO RECOGNIZING THE QUEBEC STATE ON THE INTERNATIONAL SCENE, FOLLOWING A YES VOTE IN THE REFERENDUM

There seems to be a general consensus that in the event of a massive Yes vote of Quebeckers in favor of separation (very improbable), the international community will follow the rest of Canada to the extent that the latter recognizes an independent Quebec. We can however foresee a certain number of difficulties with this recognition, since third parties might refuse to recognize an independent Quebec.

In fact, the international recognition of an independent Quebec will depend on bringing together a number of factors of a political nature.

There are thus two possible scenarios:

The first scenario is the most optimistic one, for the indépendantistes, but also the most improbable: the international community immediately recognizes an independent Quebec, following a Yes vote in a referendum on independence

This recognition would depend however on bringing together a certain number of political factors. Quebec and Canada would have to negotiate a friendly separation in which everyone agreed on splitting up assets and the debt and the demarcation of borders. Moreover, the Quebec government would have to demonstrate the effectiveness of its new state. In international law, the effectiveness of a new state is judged according to four key criteria. Does the new state have a territory? Does the new state have a population? Does the new state have organized political power? Does the new state have effective power over its territory and population? Quebec could reply quite easily to the first three criteria. But when it comes to the fourth, the international community would judge both whether Quebec had effective power independently of the federal government and in what conditions the Quebec government had obtained this power.

The second scenario is less straightforward and more plausible: the leading countries of the international community would hesitate to recognize an independent Quebec

There would be several reasons for this. The first could be related to the political context in which Quebec declared itself independent. Since the right to secede is not recognized in international law, but is a fact which the international community may or may not accept, the "heavyweight" states of the international community will not take political troubles in Quebec lightly. If Quebec decides on a unilateral declaration of independence following a referendum in which Quebec is practically cut in two (51 per cent for, 49 per cent against), it is highly unlikely that the most important countries of the international community will accept to recognize an independent Quebec.

Following the provincial elections of September 1994, in which 44.7 per cent of the electorate voted for the Parti Québécois and 44.4 per cent for the Liberal Party, the chances of a very close result in a referendum on Quebec independence do not seem at all impossible.

Needless to say, the indépendantistes claim that such a result would be sufficient to go ahead with independence. But the rest of Canada and in its train the international community could question the validity of the expression of the national will, which Jacques Parizeau himself called (May 1994) *"the democratic expression of a clear will on the part of the Quebec people"* (Lessard, 1994:B-1). On this basis, Canada could refuse to recognize an independent Quebec, in order not to threaten the economic and political stability of the country and to preserve the welfare of its population of 29 million inhabitants. Since Canada is a country with a good reputation around the world, it is probable that other countries would not wish to go against Canada's decision.

Moreover, it is possible that the borders of Quebec could be challenged (native people, border regions), creating political confusion.

The second reason why the most important countries of the international community would hesitate to recognize an independent Quebec could be a consequence of their own strategic interests.

The independence of Quebec would be a first in the modern world: a province, Quebec, with a distinct language and culture, has developed and flourished within a democratic and prosperous Canada, which is a member of the G7. Who, in this context, would have an interest in being the first to recognize an independent Quebec?

France? What strategic interest would France have in being the first to recognize Quebec, thus striking out on its own, at a time when Europe is seeking to develop common international policies? How could France justify not recognizing the merits of the indépendantiste demands of Corsicans and Bretons? Or France's overseas departments and territories (DOM-TOM), such as Martinique, Guadeloupe, New Caledonia, French Guiana, French Polynesia or St. Pierre & Miquelon? What would France's negotiating power be with DOM-TOM or regional indépendantistes, if it was the first country to recognize an independent Quebec? And the United Kingdom, with Wales and Scotland? And the United States? All industrial countries have distinct regions, made up of distinctive ethnic groups, and would therefore think twice before leaping too quickly into recognizing an independent Quebec. Particularly since Quebec is not a colony and can fulfil itself within Canada.

On the international scene, Quebec's situation is nothing like that of the former USSR or even of the former Yugoslavia, which struggled under the yoke of excessive "cultural" centralization, and authoritarian not to mention dictatorial regimes. In the former USSR, for example, the central Russian authority created strong pressures to prevent the regions from developing their own cultural autonomy. The former USSR was a federation in name alone, since all powers were concentrated in Moscow. In the former Yugoslavia, the territory was made up of different ethnic groups, held together by an authoritarian regime, within artificially-created boundaries. Some regions of Yugoslavia had a standard of living much like developing countries, while other regions lived like the industrial countries.

In the case of the former Yugoslavia, the international community has drawn lessons from the overly hasty recognition of Croatia's independence, precipitated by Germany. That recognition opened up a Pandora's Box, led to the appearance of enclaves and resulted in the conflict we all know.

CONCLUSION: THE LEGAL RIGHTS OF QUEBEC AFTER A HYPOTHETICAL YES VOTE IN A REFERENDUM ARE VAGUE AND DEBATABLE

From what appears above, we can conclude that Quebec has no automatic right to secession based on the Canadian Constitution or international jurisprudence. A Yes vote in a referendum could lead to the creation of a new Quebec state, as long as it was accepted by the rest of Canada and made legimitate by the official recognition of the international community. But the international community would probably await the acceptance of Canada and the negotiation of an eventual separation. The international community does not want to create too dangerous a precedent and has learned its lessons from Germany's overly-hasty recognition of Croatia in the former Yugoslavia, which resulted in a civil war. Therefore, if Ottawa decided not to recognize the validity of this separation, the international community could decide to consider this situation as "an internal Canadian matter" in the same way that in December 1994, it did not object to Russia's use of force in Chechnya.

On the assumption that the international community eventually decided to recognize the sovereignty of Quebec, native people could use the same procedure and even the same principles to unilaterally declare their independence, or to demand that they rejoin Canada. The principle of an "indivisible Quebec" is just as strong or as weak as the principle of an "indivisible Canada." International experience shows that once the process of division gets under way, it is very hard to stop. From a legal point of view, therefore, a Yes vote in the referendum, far from being straightforward and clear, the way indépendantistes claim, would open a Pandora's Box - the contents of which cannot now be known. It will be like navigating in troubled waters without a compass!

MYTH 10: FRENCH LANGUAGE AND CULTURE WILL BE BETTER PROTECTED IN AN INDEPENDENT QUEBEC

Context

We often hear that the French language is threatened by the English language, which is spoken everywhere in North America. According to this view, the situation of francophones can be likened to a cube of sugar slowly melting in a cup of coffee. Separation therefore offers the best way of protecting the French language and culture.

Reality is not quite so simple. But it should be noted that the indépendantistes manage to articulate the deep-seated anxiety of the majority of Quebec francophones about seeing their French cultural identity crumble and eventually disappear altogether. According to the Péquiste perspective, Quebec, a beleagured francophone island, forever at odds with Canada, risks being washed away by the Anglo-American imperialist sea. That is why the only solution for the indépendantistes is cultural and linguistic "protectionism," closing in on oneself in a unitary and unilingual state that francophones can be sure of controlling.

We will subject these ideas to critical examination, by placing them firstly in an international context and secondly in the Canadian context. The GAMMA Institute undertook a study in 1980, on behalf of the Conseil de la langue française. The experience of the last 10 years reinforces the diagnosis and conclusions the study identified, as well as the relevance of its conclusions.

THE INTERNATIONAL CONTEXT

It is vital to place the debate on the French language in the international and North American context. What can we learn from that context?

A relative weakening of French as mother tongue

There may be five times as many francophones around the world now than there were a century ago. But French as a mother tongue is losing ground, since it is essentially spoken in four countries with low birth rates: France, Belgium, Switzerland and Canada, while other languages are spreading more rapidly.

The future progress of French depends on those who speak French as a second language. According to the Atlas de la francophonie: *"The influence and expansion of French will mostly be the result of its use as a second language. French is unique among the world's great languages in this respect."*

French is no longer what it used to be: "the" language of international diplpomacy and knowledge. According to the Haut Conseil de la Francophonie, French comes 11th, in terms of the number of people speaking it. French has to be modern, it has to be used in business, the arts, culture, science and techonlogy, in order to maintain its international vitality in a ferociously competitive world, and to stand up to English, German, Chinese, Spanish and Japanese. France and Canada, both members of the G7, are the two world leaders of la Francophonie; their influence in world affairs gives great prestige to the French language.

The mobility of production factors influences the language debate

As we have seen above in the introduction, Quebec lives in an age of increasingly mobile production factors (resources, capital, labor, technology). That mobility results from the emergence of new technologies and of the multinational corporation, which operates according to its own rules.

This new economic situation has a significant impact on the language question. In a world increasingly subject to transnational flows of production factors, each country has to be as welcoming and as attractive as possible. While francophones are attracted to "America in French," non-francophones might under some conditions be dissuaded from settling in Quebec and bringing mobile capital, technology and executives with them. A society that operates in English has an advantage when it comes to industrial localization. An independent Quebec that wants to remain competitive cannot ignore that fact.

The technological revolution is bringing about an increase in the influence of English, which has become the most widely-used language in the world

On the threshold of the 21st century, it is clear that the technological revolution puts the traditional debate on language in a whole new context: thanks to the transportation revolution, everyone can travel without hindrance; the communications revolution means people can be in touch with events around the world almost as soon as they take place; and the computer revolution has opened up the "Information Superhighway."

This technological revolution has facilitated the movement of people, by means of business trips, tourism and massive emigration, which in turn has contributed to the development of a virtually planetary consciousness. Individuals now have at their finger-tips a vast array of cultural products, distributed by electronic media. A new computer universe is opening up, in which individuals can freely communicate via computer networks, without outside interference. Language itself is evolving. To use Marshall McLuhan's apt expression, we are moving from a "literary" culture to a "visual" one, and that change can have the effect of weakening national languages and undermining the quality of the spoken and written language. English, meanwhile, has established itself as the world's common denominator, thanks to the prodigious technological might of the United States and the fact that English grammar is so easy to learn.

In Canada, bilingual federal institutions and the important place reserved for the French fact have the effect of "regulating" competition from the English language, by ensuring that French is more widely used in science, business and culture. By maintaining its linguistic duality, Canada strengthens the position of French in North America. The vitality of the French language and the creativity of those who use it will do much more to defend French than any coercive language legislation. Indeed, coercive language laws are a kind of illusory defence, something like France's Maginot Line, which was easy for German aircraft and tanks to get around at the beginning of the Second World War. Nowadays, the aircraft and tanks of the war of language are to be found in high technology and in the assimilative power of English as an international language. That is why the Institut Pasteur's decision a few years ago to bring out its scientific publications in English alone is potentially more damaging for the status of French in the world - and *a fortiori* in Quebec - than bilingual signs. Writing "McDonald's" rather than "Chez McDonald" cannot destroy the French language. But any decline in the scientific "creativity" of the French language has much more serious implications for the French fact, since it brings about a rise in the cost of unilingualism for francophones, not just on the financial level, but in terms of loss of readership and loss of international influence... As a study by the GAMMA Institute showed in 1986, the real threat hanging over the French language does not come from Ottawa. It comes instead from the desire of some francophones to assimilate to English, in order to improve their chances of success in the fields of technology and business.

THE CANADIAN CONTEXT

Since the Second World War, the French language has expanded its geopolitical base in just one country in the world: Canada.

A constitutional and legislative framework that helps strengthen the "French fact"

English is being used more and more around the world, while the relative size of la Francophonie is slowly shrinking. Paradoxically, French has made big gains in Canada as a language of use, while francophones have taken their rightful place in the heart of Canada over the last 30 years.

For many years, Quebec politicians explained that French Canadians were founders of Confederation just as much as English Canadians, saying moreover that francophones had the right to government services in French and to a constitutional guarantee of the right of provincial linguistic minorities to receive instruction in their own language.

In 1969, the Parliament of Canada passed the Official Languages Act, which recognized that every community could receive government services in the official language of its choice, where the number so warranted. A few years later, in 1982, the Constitution was amended to recognize the right of provincial linguistic minorities to their own school systems. This new Constitution was denounced by Quebec's National Assembly, yet it contains a "notwithstanding" clause which Quebec has often used to restrict some rights and toughen the protection of the French language. Quebec meanwhile passed a series of laws establishing French as the official language (Bill 22 in 1974), restricting commercial signs in English, limiting access to anglophone schools (Charter of the French Language or Bill 101, passed in 1977); Bill 178 (1990). This language policy had two main consequences: it slowed the movement of "allophones" to the English-speaking community (allophone is a Quebec term meaning those people whose mother tongue is neither French nor English); and it gave added impetus to the efforts of the anglophone community to become bilingual. Since 1976, there has also been a massive emigration of anglophones from Quebec, at a time when the Quebec government has been seeking francophone immigrants.

Quebec has developed a culture of its own, with ample subsidies from national Canadian institutions

Some people like to suggest that the only way to protect French is for Quebeckers to wage a bitter struggle against the rest of Canada. In actual fact, the French language is an integral part of Canada's identity, and bilingual Canadian institutions play a key role in the development of French-language culture. Radio-Canada and the Office national du film (the respective French services of the Canadian Broadcasting Corporation and the National Film Board) are world-renowned institutions that have reflected the collective commitment of Canadians over the last half-century to the French language. Other institutions promoting French-language culture are the Canada Council, Telefilm Canada and, more recently, the Réseau de l'Information, a 24-hour French-language all-news channel on cable television, something like CBC Newsworld.

Canada's francophone creators benefit from two Canadian traditions: the arm's-length tradition, according to which institutions maintain a policy of non-interference in the content of artistic works; and the tradition of ensuring that francophone creators get a far larger share of global budgets than the actual proportion of francophones in Canada's population would seem to justify.

This is particularly striking when one analyzes Quebec's share of federal programs supporting the arts, literature and culture. According to the latest confirmed statistics (1991-92) Quebec artists, writers and creators received 37 % of all federal funds offered in cross-Canada competition in the area of culture. This excellent result is way above the 25 % "fair share" generally sought by Quebeckers. It reflects the quality of proposals submitted by Quebec's artistic community, as assessed by Canadian peer committees. The table below illustrates Quebec's performance in two major programs to support culture, namely the Canada Council (32 %) and Telefilm Canada (45 %). It should be noted that Quebec's strengths in literature and publishing help it rake in 40 % of the funds the Canada Council allocates in this sector.

$640 million or 30 % of the internal operating budget of the federal administration is spent on culture in Quebec. This high proportion can be attributed mainly to the strategic location of the National Film Board and Radio-Canada in the Montreal region.

Cross-Canada support for Quebec culture is $45 million a year higher than it would be if funding levels were determined on the basis of Quebec's share of the population.

Quebec currently receives 45 % of the budget of the Canadian government's two main cultural organizations located in Quebec (NFB and Radio-Canada). If Quebec separated from Canada, it would lose $185 million per year, on the basis of the transfer of its "fair share" of 25 %.

Francophones are well represented in the federal government and the Canadlan public service

Quebeckers have succeeded in establishing a strong presence in the federal government. Over the last 26 years, the Prime Minister of Canada has been a Quebecker (Mr. Trudeau, Mr. Mulroney, Mr. Chrétien). Quebeckers have also held key positions, whether as ministers or in the public service or in the court system.

In 1992, 28.06 % of all federal public-service positions were held by francophones, a proportion larger than francophones' share in Canada's population. In the Ottawa region, the proportion of francophones was actually 36 % (These are the latest available figures: Public Service Commission of Canada, 1992).

Francophones are well represented at the executive level in private business and Crown corporations in Canada, and the francophone control of companies operating in Quebec has increased

Up until the 1960s, francophones were under-represented at the executive level of private business and Canadian Crown corporations in Quebec. This is no longer the case. Francophones currently account for 80 % of these positions, which is close to the best possible level if one considers the ownership structure of Quebec business (Raynauld, 1990:21).

In addition, the number of companies under francophone control in Quebec has grown tremendously over the last 30 years, going from 47 % in 1961 to 65 % in 1992.

At the time of the Quiet Revolution, the number of companies under francophone control was relatively small compared to the proportion of francophones in Quebec's population. Thus, in 1961, the percentage of jobs in francophone-, anglophone- and foreign-controlled companies was 47 %, 39 % and 14 % respectively - even though francophones accounted for three-fourths of the population. This situation has improved a great deal in the last 30 years.

By 1971, there had already been a significant increase in the proportion of jobs in francophone-controlled companies, which went from 47 % to 55 %. This increase came about at the expense of companies under English Canadian control, whose share dropped from 39 % to 31 %.

In 1987, companies under francophone control gained yet more ground, now accounting for 61.6 % of all jobs. But this gain was mainly at the expense of foreign firms, whose share dropped to 8 %.

The wage gap between francophones and anglophones in Quebec has narrowed significantly over the last three decades

In 1960, at the beginning of the Quiet Revolution, the gap in employment wages of francophone and anglophone males in the Montreal region was huge - anglophones earned 51 % more than their francophone fellow citizens (Raynauld, 1990:20).

The gap between anglophone and francophone wage-earners is now practically non-existent. A 1992 study by the Conseil de la langue française shows that bilingual anglophone men earned 10 % less than bilingual francophones and 4 % less than unilingual francophones. The study compared people having the same number of years of schooling, the same professional experience and working the same number of hours each week.

CONCLUSION

Quebec is at the intersection of two trends. The first trend is worldwide: the relative weakening of French, which benefits other languages and particularly English. The second trend is Canadian: the "French fact" is growing, especially in Quebec, thanks to the combined effects of federal and provincial legislation.

Efforts to bolster the French fact operate at two levels: at the international level and the Canadian level.

THE CONSEQUENCES OF QUEBEC INDEPENDENCE

At the Canadian level, an independent Quebec would jeopardize the protection of French-language culture in Quebec

Within the Canadian framework, Quebec can pursue "francization" without worrying about the danger of isolationism or assimilation. Francophone society is recognized as a full member of Canadian society, and benefits for this reason from certain "protections," which are denounced by some people but nonetheless allow Quebec to continue along the path of francization chosen a few decades ago. This Canadian francophone society includes Quebec as well as francophones outside of Quebec, who have also in many cases managed to preserve their cultural originality. The Canadian framework acts as a kind of shock absorber, reducing external pressures.

However, if Quebec separated, it would lose this cultural "shock absorber" called Canada and would really become a beleagured francophone island surrounded by an anglophone ocean.

Separation would leave Quebec with two choices (GAMMA Institute, 1986): on the one hand, Quebec could opt for maximal francization, at the cost of economic marginalization, the way Puerto Rico chose to preserve its cultural identity at the cost of economic marginalization. Given the relative weakening of French in the world, an independent Quebec would be required to shore up its cultural "fortress" and increase its operating costs (translation of English-language world culture).

On the other hand, an independent Quebec might not be able to withstand the new pressures that Quebec independence would bring to bear on francophone culture. Paradoxically, this situation could make the assimilation of Quebec to the North American anglophone majority likelier, as was the case with Louisiana, a former French territory that chose voluntary assimilation.

At the very least, we can say that an independent Quebec's room for manoeuvre to protect French would be considerably reduced.

It is unlikely that an independent Quebec would accept economic isolation in order to ensure the survival of French. There would thus have to be a rapid recognition of the constitutional rights of the anglophone minority as well as a loosening of restrictions on the language of signs and the language of work in companies with more than 50 employees, so that Quebec could attract North America's mobile production factors (executives, companies, labor...). One can well imagine anglophone executives and labor from outside of Quebec demanding, as a precondition for settling in Quebec, access to anglophone schools currently denied them under the terms of Bill 101. In addition, in order to remain competitive in international markets, Quebec would have to vigorously promote the bilingualization of Quebeckers, who would have to work more than ever in English.

Faced with these constraints, Quebeckers living in an independent Quebec might one day opt for voluntary assimilation to the North American anglophone majority, something that is currently unthinkable within the Canadian framework.

At the international level: Quebec will find it easier to defend the French language as part of Canada, a member of the G7 and considered a "francophone country" by la Francophonie, than as a country with just 7 milion inhabitants isolated from the rest of North America

The protection of French also requires it to be defended on the international scene. Francophone countries have to work at increasing the vitality of the French language, by boosting the number of people who speak the language and increasing its "degree of modernity," that is, the use made of French in business, the arts, culture, science, technology....

At the international level, this defence will depend on an alliance of francophone forces. Clearly, the greater a country's economic and demographic clout, the greater its impact in promoting its language will be. France plays an important role in la Francophonie. So does Canada, since it is a member of the G7, and is recognized by francophone organizations as a "francophone country." In fact, France and Canada are the only two large and prosperous countries of la Francophonie, the other countries being either small (Belgium and Luxemburg) or states of limited influence with minimal francophone populations (Romania, Senegal, Haiti, Laos, Morocco, etc.) It is important for the world francophone community to have two members among the G7, since the only way to stop the decline of French in the world is to have prosperous and large francophone countries working to increase its vitality.

By separating from Canada's "francophonie," Quebec will weaken its ability to promote the francophone cause worldwide.

Canada acts as an institutional "cushion" for Quebec, helping it shield its French language and culture from world pressures. Quebec has to stand up to the world tendency of French to lose ground to other languages, among them English. The combined effect of provincial and federal policies has boosted French in Quebec, by increasing its vitality and the place of francophones in Canadian institutions. The federal policy of official bilingualism is supported by the vast majority of francophones and recognizes French as one of Canada's official languages, on an equal footing with the English language. Quebec's separation from the rest of Canada would threaten the vitality of French language and culture in North America, since Quebec would lose fundamental advantages and would have to either isolate itself economically or soft-pedal its francization policies, in order to protect its language.

CONCLUSION: PARADOXICALLY, QUEBEC INDEPENDENCE THREATENS THE SURVIVAL OF QUEBEC'S FRANCOPHONE CULTURE

Quebec is caught between two trends. The first trend is that French is losing ground worldwide, since French as a mother tongue is mainly spoken in four countries with low birth rates. Meanwhile, the use of other languages such as Spanish and Chinese is growing faster, and English reigns supreme as the first language used in the fields of science, technology, business and international affairs.

The second trend is a Canadian one: French has become stronger in Quebec because of its increased vitality and the place of francophones in Canadian institutions. The policy of official bilingualism, a federal policy supported by the majority of francophones, recognizes French as one of Canada's two official languages, on an equal footing with English. This is the most significant "territorial gain" made by the French language over the last half-century, anywhere in the world.

Far from being a threat for the French language, Canada actually offers protection from the worldwide trend that sees French losing ground.

Canada acts as an institutional "cushion" for Quebec, helping it shield French language and culture from worldwide pressures on French.

By separating, Quebec would lose fundamental advantages.

Quebec independence therefore goes against the interests of the vitality of Quebec's francophone culture and threatens its survival.

PART II

SUMMARY
AND CONCLUSIONS

THE TEN MYTHS IN PERSPECTIVE

A careful analysis of the arguments used most frequently to support Quebec independence turns up major flaws in every single case. The ten myths are just that - pure and unadulterated myths. They hinder the real debate we need to have, about both Quebec separation and what it would entail. It is vital for Quebeckers to know what is at stake, since they will have to accept not just a lower standard of living in a separate Quebec, but also a Quebec whose "sovereignty" is diminished. In the summary table (see pages 188-189), we summarize each of the pro-independence arguments and logical responses to those arguments.

1. We are told that Canadian federalism is rigid and unchanging. However, the experience of the last 130 years shows on the contrary that federalism evolves a lot, that it adapts to new circumstances, allows new redistributions of power and introduces innovative elements. In fact, some people complain that Canadian federalism is too flexible, since they prefer the stability of the American system. The rules of the game of Canadian federalism are always being renegotiated and frequently do evolve. That may not always be to the advantage of Canadian federalism, but it has proven necessary to respond to the needs of a country that is culturally and economically asymmetrical.

2. Some people claim, without providing either figures or proof, that Canada's constitutional problem is caused by the supposedly excessive centralization of the federal State, which voraciously invades provincial powers and jurisdictions. There is not much to this claim. Canada is much less centralized than its two partners in the North American Free Trade Agreement, the United States and Mexico. Canada is said to be the least-centralized country after Switzerland. In actual

fact, Switzerland is more centralized than Canada in many ways. Our country is thus the most decentralized federation in the world at the moment. Imagining that Canada will be saved by means of greater decentralization, or of "sovereignty-association," or even by the sort of "deconfederation" supported by some quasi-separatists in Western Canada, is a way of proposing fanciful solutions to a totally imaginary problem. There is a serious flaw in the Canadian system: the 11 governments of the country do not coordinate or pool their efforts, which results in waste and contradictory policies. Canadians should harmonize their efforts the way Europeans do, insetad of weakening their country through useless confrontations.

3. According to the third fashionable argument, federalism costs Quebeckers a lot. And when people can't find any objective facts to back up this claim, they do as Jacques Parizeau did in November 1994 when he said that "Canada's generosity hurts Quebec." This curious argument merits further study and will certainly appeal to those Albertans who see Quebec as the spoilt child of the federation and a province that doesn't deserve any more gifts! There are no grounds for saying that Quebec pays more to the federal government than it receives from that government. The figures are clear. In Canada, three provinces are on the giving end (British Columbia, Alberta and Ontario) while seven are on the receiving end of federal dollars. The Maritime provinces are the leading beneficiaries of these transfers, but Quebec is also an important beneficiary and there is no doubt that Quebec has received more over the last 50 years than it has given.

Having said that, it is important to challenge the argument according to which Quebec should only stay in Canada as long as federalism is "profitable." A federation is more than a game, where some people can only be kept happy by exploiting other people. Like mariage or friendship, a federation has to offer benefits to all parties - benefits that go well beyond straight dollars and cents. In a federation, everyone wins or everyone loses. All provinces should be able to get more out of the federation than they put in, because of the synergies created by the federation. The *raison d'être* of a federation is undermined if people adopt the ledger-sheet approach - and if nobody believes that unity is strength and that greater things can be accomplished by joining forces with their partners. The federal system is certainly the best way to face up to the complex nature of modern society.

Moreover, Canada has managed to develop unique values that go well beyond the federal system as such. These values help distinguish Canada from its powerful neighbor to the south, and also ensure Canada's autonomy.

4. The fourth myth has to do with the difficult problem of the public debt, since Canada and Quebec are already heavily in debt. The combination of this double debt load in an independent Quebec could prove fatal to the economic health of both parties, Canada and Quebec. No plausible scenario leads one to believe that Quebec separation would improve the State's finances. The debt burden will be split up at the negotiating table - but Quebec will have already played the card of threatening to separate from Canada. After independence, a very difficult period is foreseeable, because of the combination of higher interest rates and the division of the debt. A lot of Quebec's debt is already held abroad. Quebec's vulnerability will be even greater and more distressing, if one adds to "foreign" creditors those non-Quebec Canadian creditors holding Quebec's debt (federal and provincial).

5. As for the view that the Quebec-Canada economic union will continue after independence, this view betrays in our opinion a lack of understanding of the forces at play. Canada no longer needs Quebec the way it did during the period of the 1980 referendum, because of NAFTA and the effects of globalization. The same argument can be applied to Quebec, with the proviso that the smaller size of Quebec makes it

more dependent on the Canadian market than the other way around. The idea of an economic union implies the harmonization of economic policies, including fiscal and monetary policies. Canada's existing economic union is incomplete as it is. It is hard to see how and why Quebec independence would improve the situation. A free-trade zone would probably be created by Quebec and Canada, along the lines of NAFTA, but it would not more integrated than that. And if the monetary union is maintained, it will be in less advantageous conditions than Quebec currently enjoys - unless the rest of Canada decides to be particularly generous towards a Quebec that has just separated....

6. As far as NAFTA is concerned, it is hard to see why, at a time when markets are expanding, the United States and Mexico would block Quebec's accession. But that is not the real question. A more subtle and relevant question is what the conditions of Quebec's accession would be. Our analysis leads us to conclude that these new conditions would be much less advantageous than they currently are, and that Quebec would have to give up many well-established acquired rights, unless once again its partners in NAFTA (including Canada) decided to be particularly altruistic towards Quebec.

7. When it comes to competitiveness, Quebec independence would first of all call into question the use of interventionist policies (Quebec Inc.) that are acceptable within the framework of the Canadian federation, but would be considered violations of international agreements. Quebec would have to accept a loss of control in this area as well. Moreover, the federal government will no longer be mandated to protect Quebec's interests. Without Ottawa's mediation, Quebec's economic relationship with Ontario will be marked by more aggressive competition than it now is. People who believe Quebec would automatically win out in this sort of relationship are naïvely optimistic.

8. On the complex subject of unemployment, it is hard to accept the argument that an independent Quebec could better attain its objective of full employment than it can at present. The level of employment is determined by the pressures and disruption unleashed and fed by globalization, as well as technological change. An independent Quebec will not be spared those pressures. The only way for Quebec to succeed in creating full employment is to shut itself off from the outside world, and opt for artificial employment, financed by higher budget deficits and various protectionist measures. Since such a scenario is improbable, an independent Quebec will be as vulnerable if not more vulnerable to current trends affecting unemployment worldwide. The solution to the problem of employment is to avoid the global trend of the lowest common denominator, by developing international agreements that harmonize working conditions, without re-sorting to protectionism. Why would Quebec be any more successful in this respect than large countries already in existence?

9. In addition, the Parti Québécois and Bloc Québécois claim that the principle of self-determination means that a Yes in the referendum would allow Quebec to unilaterally declare independence. Neither the Parti Québécois nor the Bloc Québécois can find any grounds for such a claim in Canadian or in international legal texts. The Canadian Constitution remains the law of the land until proven otherwise, and contains no clause allowing a province to secede. Interna-tional law does not recognize the right to secede, except for colonies (or comparable territories). The eventual success of Quebec independence will therefore depend on whether it is recognized by Canada and by the international commu-nity. The international community will be extremely cau-tious, before launching into this kind of adventure in North America. The international community will not legitimize the new situation until it is ready to do so, and only if Canada

accepts the secession (following a massive Yes vote and after protracted negotiations).

The current boundaries of Quebec are not cast in concrete since native people can also invoke their own independence using the same arguments as Quebec (referendum, control of a territory, appeals to international sympathy, etc.) They can also request to remain a part of Canada.

For all these reasons, it is unrealistic to suppose that a unilateral declaration of independence following St. Jean Baptiste Day celebrations would immediately be accepted by one and all. Everything will be on the table, including the boundaries of Quebec.

10. Finally, the question of the protection of the French language and culture: the need to protect the French language is the argument most frequently used in favor of independence. Indeed, the preferred instrument of the indépendantistes seems to be independence accompanied by coercive language legislation. Unfortunately, once again, the geopolitical forces at play do not favor this position. The political and economic withdrawal of an independent Quebec would weaken the vitality of the French fact in North America. Quebec would no longer have the benefit of Canada, a protective "cushion" shielding it from the worldwide growth of English language and culture. Quebec would no longer benefit from Canadian mechanisms which institutionalize and protect the French language. As a result, Quebec would be the lone defender of French in North America, in an English-speaking and Spanish-speaking ocean. We would be facing the assimilative power of technology and the global economy, and could thus fear, with reason, for the very survival of the French language in North America. If Canada didn't exist, Quebec would have an interest in inventing it.

A MISLEADING KIND OF SOVEREIGNTY

This summary of weaknesses in the panoply of indépendantiste arguments leads us back to the questions raised in the introductory chapter at the beginning of this book: what kind of sovereignty is being offered to us in an independent Quebec and how would the lot of Quebeckers be improved? We will answer these questions by encouraging the reader to look at the integrating table. Clearly, the indépendantiste position is hiding behind linguistic and semantic ambiguity surrounding the word "sovereignty" - ambiguity that may well be intentional.

Can this "sovereignty" be limited strictly to the symbols of independence? The Parti Québécois' vision emphasizes rituals, popular festivals and ceremonial. The head of the government has an official residence, the country has a flag, a national anthem, a Quebec passport (in addition to a Canadian passport), and foreign diplomatic representation. The new country has its own seat at the International Monetary Fund, the World Bank, UNESCO, the OECD, the United Nations. St. Jean Baptiste Day becomes the day of national independence. This symbolic sovereignty seems to correspond to the distinct character of Quebec society. The mere fact of declaring that Quebec is sovereign after a referendum will be enough to prove that Quebeckers are masters of their destiny, even if an act of reconfederation has to be signed with Canada a few days later....

But then there are the real indépendantistes - who want the kind of real sovereignty that means exercising substantial powers. Mercantilists such as Montchrétien, Richelieu and Colbert claimed that real sovereignty was the power to issue one's own currency and thus control monetary policy. Several monetarists share this view. The power to issue one's own currency is the sovereign's real power. Depriving oneself of this power means limiting one's sovereignty. That is exactly what the indépendantiste project does by abandoning an independent currency, and promising to stay in the Canadian monetary zone and to use the Canadian dollar. As we have seen in the chapter on the Canadian economic union, this is a prudent course to adopt, but it also considerably diminishes the sovereignty of an independent Quebec, by limiting its power within the monetary zone.

Real sovereignty is the ability to defend oneself. As things stand, Canada could hardly defend itself if it were attacked by its sole American neighbor. Quebec would be even less able to deter aggression by the United States, the rest of Canada or even a foreign aggressor, unless Quebec invested massively in a Quebec army, which is improbable. An independent Quebec would therefore rely on the security umbrellas of Canada and/or the United States.

An independent Quebec would run smack into the wall of planetary interdependence. In fact, there is no truly indépendantiste party in Quebec, since real sovereignty is such an improbable scenario. The indépendantiste movement is polite and convivial; it is grounded in vague legal concepts and does not inflame passions overly much. Listening to indépendantistes, it seems as if it would be enough to rejig the *status quo,* change a few symbols, adjust the laws, restructure the hierarchy of laws and regulations - and call the whole thing "sovereignty."

THE DELUSION OF INDEPENDENCE

Some people will therefore ask why Quebeckers shouldn't choose the inoffensive and purely sentimental option of sovereignty. Why not proclaim Quebec independence and move on right afterwards to reconfederation with the rest of Canada, with a single currency, the same tax system, strategic alliances with other provinces, etc.? This scenario may seem attractive at first sight, but it just won't stand up to critical examination.

The *raison d'être* of Canada cannot be economic alone. If Canada's political dimension is torn away, if its social project and ideals are abandoned, there won't be enough reasons left to maintain a country as large as half of a continent, inhabited by only 29 million people concentrated in a 200-kilometre-wide swathe of land along the American border. Economic imperatives would impose continental free trade and eventually a merger with the United States. But the political, cultural and social characteristics of the Canadian project make up its *raison d'être*. Canadians of all backgrounds recognize the distinct character of Canada, compared to the United States, and they appreciate Canadian values. It is hard to define the "Canadian identity," but there is a kind of socio-cultural and political cement binding Canadians together. And everyone, francophone as much as anglophone, wants to hold on to his or her Canadian passport.

By separating, Quebec would destroy this socio-political project and would call everything into question. The monolithic homogeneity of English Canada is a myth created in Quebec. If Quebec can leave, why will British Columbia stay? Can the rest of Canada survive politically, if half of its population and just about the absolute majority of members of the House of Commons are from Ontario? Once the Maritime provinces are geographically separated from the rest of anglophone Canada, will they continue to be the poor cousins of the country, on the receiving end of transfer payments? All of this remains unclear. It is highly likely that the rest of Canada would not survive very long after Quebec's departure. It is possible that political agreements could be negotiated with the United States. On this assumption, the rest of Canada, the secure partner an independent Quebec is counting on, will no longer be there. That partner may splinter, and the Quebec republic may discover in 10 or 15 years that it has become a marginal player next to the Unted States of North America.

That is why the idea of a sovereign and independent Quebec is so misleading. Even if sovereignty is only symbolic, it will reduce Quebec's real power, and will accelerate the political collapse of Canada. Quebec will actually lose influence by seeking to obtain extra powers when geopolitical conditions are working against it. That is why the people who are fighting to keep Quebec within the Canadian political union are acting like the true friends of Quebec's interests - and not those who are encouraging Quebec to become independent.

Is a separate, weakened country what Quebeckers really want? Do they want the pleasure of declaring independence, if it means giving up the control levers that have already made Quebec a "sovereign" distinct province in many areas and influential in many others? Do they want to depend totally and permanently on foreign countries, when it comes to establishing economic and social policies? Are they ready to put the survival of their distinct francophone character at risk and see their standard of living drop for an indefinite period of time? We don't think so.

Quebec has always had important political levers, within Canada. As a result, the custom of voting as a bloc for the winning federal party has helped Quebec exert considerable political influence in Canada. Since 1968, the Prime Ministers of Canada have all been Quebeckers, if one leaves aside the short terms of office of Joe Clark, John Turner and Kim Campbell. In 1993, Quebec abandoned its habit of voting for the winner, opting to elect 54 MPs of the Bloc Québécois instead. In so doing, Quebec abandoned one of its most powerful political tools: control of the federal House of Commons, which reached a high point during the era of Mr. Trudeau and Mr. Mulroney. Now Ontario dominates the federal government, since 98 of its 98 MPs sitting in Ottawa are Liberals.

In addition, Quebec has long articulated the nationalist vision of a distinct society, whether it was under Maurice Duplessis, Jean Lesage, Daniel Johnson senior, Robert Bourassa, René Lévesque, Pierre-Marc Johnson or Daniel Johnson junior. As a result, Quebec has always obtained a lot. By acceding to independence, Quebec would give up any chance of winning more. And with a weakened power of negotiation and a smaller GNP and population than other players at the bargaining table, Quebec would be trying to strike a better deal, by reassociating with the rest of Canada! This strategy seems so bungled that if Clausewitz or Machiavelli ever returned from the grave to advise the Quebec government, they would reject it outright! Not only would Quebec independence destroy Canada, but it would above all weaken Quebec itself!

We summarize our analysis of the project of Quebec independence with the two following statements, which express the essence of our thesis:

---

1. The "sovereignty" being proposed by the Parti Québécois is essentially a delusion. To the extent that it is real, the Parti Québécois' vision of sovereignty is unfortunately not feasible, because of the growing interdependence of countries.

And to the extent that it is feasible, this vision of sovereignty is unfortunately not real.

2. Even a symbolic sort of "sovereignty" that is harmless in apparence, is not desirable: all the scenarios, even the most optimistic ones, demonstrate paradoxically that Quebec would end up being weaker. By being symbolically sovereign outside of Canada, Quebec would lose a great part of the influence it currently exerts within Canada, and would lose full control of its destiny. The best aspects of the indépendantiste social project can be implemented within Canada.

By choosing a misleading form of sovereignty, Quebec runs the risk of making a useless strategic error — an error from which there is no return.

SUMMARY TABLE

MYTHS	BACK TO REALITY
1. Federalism is rigid and unchanging	The current system is flexible and develops by stages. We have seen several changes since 1867 as well as a capacity to adapt to new circumstances.
2. The Canadian state is too centralized.	Canada is much less centralized that its neighbor, the United States, and to some extent even less centralized than Switzerland. This means our federation is the least centralized in the world.
3. Federalism costs Quebeckers a lot.	Quebec has benefited handsomely from its membership in the Canadian federation. The three "have" provinces (Ontario, Alberta and British Columbia) subsidize the "have-not" provinces, like Quebec, ensuring that they can offer the same quality of services.
4. An independent Quebec will easily get out of paying the Canadian debt.	An independent Quebec will have to take on a considerable share of the Canadian debt, in addition to its own debt load. It will thus be the most indebted country of the OECD, per capita.
5. After independence, the Quebec-Canada economic union is in the bag.	Because of NAFTA, the rest of Canada now needs Quebec less than in 1980, and vice versa. A Quebec-Canada economic union is unlikely. But a quasi-free-trade zone between the two could be created.
6: Getting Quebec into NAFTA will be a cinch	Quebec will probably get into NAFTA, but it will be in less favorable conditions than currently exist, since Quebec's negotiating clout will be reduced.

7: Quebec will be more competitive as an independent country than if it stays in the Canadian federation	An independent Quebec will no longer be able to count on its membership in the Canadian federation to maintain and improve its competitiveness. With less room for manoeuvre, it will be up against Ontario and the Rest of Canada, both of which will be less willing to make concessions.
8: Full employment will be easy to bring about in an independent Quebec	Because of globalization and technological change, among other things, an independent Quebec will have less room for manoeuvre than Quebec now has within the Canadian federation, to bring about full employment.
9: The Quebec people have the right to self-determination	This debatable position is backed up neither by jurisprudence nor expert legal opinion. If Quebec declares its independence, it will have to obtain the recognition of the international community, and will not be able to refuse the right of native people to remain in Canada.
10: French language and culture will be better protected in an independent Quebec	French would be threatened in an independent Quebec. It would be isolated in North America (even if contacts were maintained with francophones outside of Quebec), and separated from Canada, which acts as a cushion, shielding it from the worldwide expansion of English.

SELECTED BIBLIOGRAPHY

Akyeampong, E. (1993). *La population active,* catalogue 71-001 (Ottawa: Statistique Canada).

Akyeampong, E. (1987). *La population active,* catalogue 71-001 (Ottawa: Statistique Canada).

Annuaire du Canada (1994). (Ottawa: Statistique Canada).

Baril, J. (1983). *Le marché du travail, Québec* (Québec: Ministère de la Main-d'œuvre et de sécurité du revenu) no 67-75.

Beaudoin, G-A. (1982). *Le partage des pouvoirs* (Ottawa: Éditions de l'Université d'Ottawa).

Beaudoin, G-A. (1994a). «Le statu quo existe-t-il vraiment (1): le fédéralisme canadien n'a jamais cessé d'évoluer au fil des époques», *La Presse,* 29 septembre, p. B-3.

Beaudoin, G-A. (1994b). «Le statu quo existe-t-il vraiment (2): la Cour suprême au secours des politiciens», *La Presse,* 30 septembre, p. B-3.

Beaulnes, A. (1994). «Science, media, politique», *Cité libre,* juillet-août, p. 7-15.

Bélanger-Campeau - *Commission sur l'avenir politique et constitutionnel du Québec* (1991).Eléments de l'analyse économique pertinents à la révision du statut politique et constitutionnel du Québec , Document de travail, no 1. (Québec: Les Publication officielles).

Bellemare, D., Poulin-Simon, L. (1983). *Le plein-emploi: pourquoi?,* (Québec: Presses de l'université du Québec).

Bercuson, D., Cooper, B. (1991). *Deconfederation: Canada without Québec* (Toronto: Key Porter Books).

Bernier, G. (1992). dans *Bilan québécois du fédéralisme canadien,* sous la direction de Francois Rocher (Montréal: VLB).

Bird, R. (1986). *Federal Finance in a Comparative Perspective* (Toronto: Canadian Tax Foundation).

Bouchard, L., éd. (1993). *Un nouveau parti pour l'étape décisive* (Montréal: Fides).

Bureau de Statistique du Québec (1990-1991). *Le Québec et ses régions* (Québec: Bureau de statistique du Québec).

Bureau de Statistique du Québec (1992). *Le Québec et ses régions: Montréal* (Québec: Bureau de statistique du Québec).

Buchanan A. (1992). «Quebec Secession and Native Territorial Rights», *The Network,* March, p. 2.

CEE (1981). *La politique régionale: Principes d'égalité et de développement harmonieux des régions* (Bruxelles: CEE).

Clavet, A. (1994). «L'indépendance pour faire quoi?» *Cité Libre,* novembre-décembre, p. 17-21.

Comité consultatif sur le développement de la région de Montréal. *(1987). Rapport Picard,* (Montréal: Ville de Montréal).

Commission de formation professionnelle de la main-d'œuvre (1987). *Région Métropolitaine de Montréal: Portrait socio-économique* (Montréal: Commission de Formation professionnelle de la Main-d'œuvre).

Commission de la fonction publique du Canada (1992). *Rapport annuel* (Ottawa: Commission de la fonction publique du Canada).

Commission de l'emploi et de l'immigration du Canada (1988). *Perspectives de l'économie et du marché du travail, île de Montréal* (Montréal: Commission de l'Emploi et de l'immigration du Canada).

Congress of the United States (1987). *The Constitution of the United States of America, Analysis and Interpretation.* Doc. no 99-16, p. 151-161.

Conseil des Affaires sociales, Québec (1989). *Rapport sur le développement social et démographique,* (Québec: Les Publications officielles).

Conseil des Affaires sociales, Québec (1990). *Agir ensemble* (Québec: Les Publications officielles).

Conseil du Trésor du Canada, Secrétariat (1991). *Chevauchement et dédoublement des programmes fédéraux et provinciaux,.* (Ottawa: Conseil de Trésor du Canada, Secrétariat).

Conseil national de Bien-être social (1994). *Profil de la pauvreté: Québec,* (Ottawa: Conseil national de Bien-être social).

Conseil privé (1992) *Répertoire des ententes administratives* (Ottawa: Approvisionnements et services).

Courchêne, T.J. (1991). *In Praise of Renewed Federalism* (Toronto: C.D. Howe Institute).

Cournoyer, M. (1992). « Les caractéristiques principales des personnes à bas revenu au Québec», *Interventions économiques,* no 19, p. 93-107.

Dehousse, R. (1991). *Fédéralisme et relations internationales* (Bruxelles: Ed. Bruyland).

Dion, S. (1993). «Les députés du Bloc devraient s'engager à démissionner si le projet péquiste échoue», *La Presse,* 13 octobre, p. B-3.

Economic Council of Canada (1991). *A Joint Venture: The Economics of Constitutional Options,* Twenty-Eighth Annual Review, (Ottawa: Supply and Services, Canada).

Economist (1993). «Not So Amicable», April 17, p. 50-51.

Economist Intelligence Unit (1992). Country Report: Czechoslovakia. no 4.

Economist Intelligence Unit (1993a). *Country Report: Czechoslovakia.* no 1.

*Economist Intelligence Unit (*1993b). *Country Report: Czechoslovakia.* no 2.

Economist Intelligence Unit (1993c). *Country Report: Czechoslovakia.* no 3.

Economist Intelligence Unit (1993d). *Country Report: Czechoslovakia.* no 4.

Economist Intelligence Unit (1994a). *Country Report: Czechoslovakia.* no 1.

Economist Intelligence Unit (1994b). *Country Report: Czechoslovakia.* no 2.

Economist Intelligence Unit (1994c). *Country Report: Czechoslovakia.* no 3.

European Economy (1990). October.

Finklestein, N., Vegh, G. (1992). «The Separation of Québec and the Constitution of Canada», *Background Studies of the York University Constitutional Reform Project, Study #2* (Toronto: York University).

Fontaine, M. (1994) «Le fédéralisme empêche le Québec de se sortir d'un endettement chronique, soutient Le Hir», *La Presse,* 2 novembre, p. B-4.

Fournier, A. (1991). «Le Rapport Arpin: la réponse trompeuse», *Cité Libre,* novembre. p. 12-14.

Fournier A. et L.- P. Rochon (sous la dir.) (1992) *Thèse et foutaises. Défis pour une nouvelle génération* (Montréal: L'Étincelle; Breaking with Conventional Wisdom: Robert Davies Publishing).

Fournier, A., Tombs, G. (1992). «The Fall and Rise of the French Language», *World Monitor,* May.

Fournier, A., Tombs, G. (1993). «Oh? Canada?», *World Monitor,* January, p. 42-46.

Fournier, A. (1994a). «Pourquoi Washington et Paris n'ont pas dit Oui à Lucien Bouchard», *La Presse,* 2 juin, p. B-3.

Fournier, A. (1994b). «La force tranquille du Canada», *Politique Internationale,* Printemps, p. 305-317.

Fournier, E (1995). «La Conférence des États américains», *Les Affaires et la vie,* Radio-Canada, 2 janvier.

Franck, T.M. et al. (1992). *«L'intégrité territoriale du Québec dans l'hypothèse de l'accession à la souveraineté»* (Québec: Commission d'étude des questions afférentes à l'accession du Québec à la souveraineté»).

Government Finance Statistics (1993). (Washington: International Monetary Fund).

Ha, T. Thanh. (1994). «Québec's borders are safe within Canada», *The Montreal Gazette,* 25 mai, p. A-1, A-2.

Hogg, P. (1992). *Constitutional Law of Canada* (Toronto:Carswell).

Hughes, R. (1982). *Constitutions of The Countries of the World: Switzerland* (New York: Oceania Publications).

Institut Gamma (1986). *Prospective de la langue française au Québec:* rapport pour le Conseil de la langue française, sous la direction de Kimon Valaskakis (Québec: Editeur officiel du Québec).

ISOGROUP Consultants (1992) «Québec-Canada 2000. The potential for excellence and the spectre of mediocrity», *Report to the Montreal Board of Trade*

Interventions économiques (1989). «La flexibilité du travail et de l'emploi». no 19, dossier thématique.

Jackson. G. (1988). «Mesures et concepts supplémentaires du chômage», *La population active,* catalogue 71-528 (Ottawa: Statistique Canada).

Kloti, U. (1988). «Political Ideals, Financial Interests, and Intergovernmental Relations», *Government and Opposition,* Vol. 23, Winter, p. 91-102.

Lamonde P. (1990). *La transformation de l'économie montréalaise* (Montréal: INRS-Urbanisation).

Langlois. R. (1991). *S'appauvrir dans un pays riche* (Montréal: Éd. St-Martin).

Laurendeau-Dunton (1965). *Rapport préliminaire de la Commission royale d'enquête sur le bilinguisme et le biculturalisme* (Ottawa: Queen's Printer).

Leslie, P. (1991). *The European Community: A Political Model for Canada?* (Ottawa:Supply and Services).

Lessard, D. (1994). «Référendum: Québec n'a pas de permission à demander, dit Parizeau», *La Presse,* 26 mai, p. B-1.

Mackenzie, E. (1994). *Privatopia: Homeowner Associations & the Rise of Residential Private Government* (New Haven: Yale University Press).

Magnet, J.E. (1994).«Crise constitutionnelle à l'horizon», *Le Devoir*, 18 juin. p. A-11.

Mallory, J. (1984). *The Structure of Canadian Government* (Toronto: Gage).

Ministère des Finances du Canada (1994 a). *Les dépenses fédérales* (Ottawa: Ministère des Finances du Canada).

Ministère des Finances du Canada (1994 b). *Les recettes publiques* (Ottawa: Ministère des Finances du Canada).

Ministère des Finances du Canada (1994 c). *Transferts fédéraux aux provinces* (Ottawa: Ministère des Finances du Canada).

Ministère des Finances du Canada, Direction des relations fédérales-provinciales et de la politique sociale (1994d). *Données sur les transferts fédéraux vers les provinces* (Ottawa: Ministère des Finances du Canada).

Ministère des Finances du Québec (1994). *Budget 1994-1995* (Québec: Ministère des Finances du Québec).

Ministère de l'Industrie et du commerce (1990). *Les PME au Québec, état de la situation* (Québec: Ministère de l'industrie et du commerce).

Ministère de l'Industrie et du commerce (1992a). *Les PME au Québec, état de la situation* (Québec: Ministère de l'Industrie et du commerce).

Ministère de l'Industrie, du commerce et de la technologie (1992b). *Vers une société à valeur ajoutée* (Québec: Ministère de l'Industrie, du commerce et de la technologie).

Ministère de l'Industrie et du Commerce (1993). *Les PME au Québec, état de la situation* (Québec: Ministère de l'Industrie et du commerce).

Ministère de la Main-d'œuvre et de sécurité du revenu (1989). *La PME au Québec, une manifestation de dynamisme économique* (Québec: Ministère de la Main-d'œuvre et de securité du revenu).

Ministère de la Main-d'œuvre et de sécurité du revenu (1992). *Surplus et pénurie de la main-d'œuvre au Québec et ses régions* (Québec: Les Publications officielles).

Ministère de la Main-d'œuvre et de sécurité du revenu (1993). *Le bulletin régional sur le marché du travail* (Québec: Les Publications officielles).

Ministère du Travail du Québec (1992). *Les relations du travail en 1991* (Québec: Ministère du travail du Québec).

Office de Planification et développement du Québec (1988). *Bilan socio-économique de Montréal* (Québec: Les Publications officielles).

Office de Planification et Développement du Québec (1990). *Les régions administratives du Québec,* (Québec: Les Publications du Québec).

Orban, E. (1984). *La dynamique de la centralisation dans l'État fédéral* (Montréal: Québec/Amérique).

Parti québécois, (1994). *Des idées pour mon pays: programme du Parti québécois* (Montréal: Parti québécois).

Pelletier, M. (1992). «Le processus de négociation dans les secteurs public et privé», *Les relations de travail* (Québec: Ministère du travail du Québec).

Pepin-Robarts (1979). *Se retrouver: observations et recommandations,* (Ottawa: Commission de l'Unité canadienne).

Polèse, M. (1988). «La transformation des économies urbaines: tertiarisation, délocalisation et croissance économique», *Cahiers des recherches sociologiques,* no 11, automne.

Rapport Allaire. Commission constitutionnelle du Parti libéral du Québec (1991). *Un Québec libre de ses choix* (Québec: Parti libéral du Québec).

Raynauld, A. (1990). *Les enjeux économiques de la souveraineté* (Montréal: Université de Montréal, Département de sciences économiques).

Rémillard, G. (1980). *Le fédéralisme canadien* (Montréal: Québec/Amérique).

Richardson, R. (1994). *The Public Debt of an Independent Quebec* (Vancouver: Fraser Institute).

Ritchie, G. (1991). «Putting Humpty Dumpty Together Again: Free Trade, the Breakup Scenario», dans *Broken Links: Trade Relations after a Quebec Secession* (Toronto: C.D. Howe Institute).

Robertson, G. (1994). «Accession à la souveraineté: le PQ manque de réalisme», *Le Soleil,* 22 juin. p. A-15.

Robitaille, L-B. (1994). «Québec proclamera unilateralement son indépendance si Ottawa fait traîner les choses—Lucien Bouchard», *La Presse,* 20 mai, p. A-1, A-2.

Royal Bank of Canada (1992). *Unity or disunity: An economic analysis of the benefits and the costs* (Montreal: Economics Department Royal Bank of Canada).

Smiley, D. (1984). «Public Sector Politics, Modernization: The Canadian and American Experience», *Publius,* Vol. 14, no 1, Winter, p. 39-60.

Statistique Canada (1990). *Industries manufacturières du Canada: niveaux national et provincial,* catalogue 31-203 (Ottawa: Statistique Canada).

Statistique Canada (1993). «Les flux du commerce interprovincial des biens et des services», *Le Quotidien,* catalogue 11-001F, 24 août, (Ottawa: Statistique Canada) .

Statistique Canada (1994). *Enquête mensuelle sur les industries manufacturières,* catalogue 31-101, juin (Ottawa: Statistique Canada)

Tremblay, D.G. (1991). *Le Québec et ses régions* (Québec: Ed. S-Martin).

Turp, D. (1992). «Québec's Democratic Right to Self determination: A Critical and Legal Reflection» dans *Tangled Web: Legal Aspects of Deconfederation* (Toronto: C.D. Howe Institute).

Union des Municipalités du Québec. (1991). *Manuel de formation* (Québec: Union des Municipalités du Québec).

Valaskakis, K. (1980). *Le Québec et son destin international* (Montréal, Les Quinze)

Valaskakis, K. (1990). *Le Canada des années 90: effrondrement ou renaissance* (Montréal: Transcontinental).

Valaskakis, K. (1992). «L'entreprise apatride et les politiques de l'État»,dans *Rechercher les convergences: les actes du colloque d'Aylmer,* sous la direction de Jean Chretien (Hull: Éditions Voyageur).

Valaskakis, K. (1994). «Wanted: a GATT agreement that covers workers», *The Globe and Mail,* April 22.

Ville de Montréal (1991). *Partenaires dans le développement économique des quartiers* (Montréal:Ville de Montréal).

Walker, M. (1994). *Government Spending Facts* (Vancouver: Fraser Institute).

Wall Street Journal (1995) *Federalism & Outloook,* 3 janvier.

William, S. A. (1992). «International Legal effects of Secession by Québec», *Background Studies of the York University Constitutional Reform Project, Study #3* (Toronto: York University).

NEWSPAPERS AND MAGAZINES USED
SYSTEMATICALLY IN THE RESEARCH FOR THIS BOOK:

L'Actualité
Le Devoir
La Presse
Cité Libre
The Globe and Mail
· *Maclean's*
New York Times
Options politiques (IRPP)
The Economist
The Montreal Gazette
The Toronto Star
The Wall Street Journal